The Widow
Down by the Brook

A Memoir of a Time Gone By

Mary MacNeill

Scribner

SCRIBNER
1230 Avenue of the Americas
New York, NY 10020

Designed by Brooke Zimmer
Set in Monotype Sabon
Manufactured in the United States of America

1   3   5   7   9   10   8   6   4   2

Library of Congress Cataloging-in-Publication Data

MacNeill, Mary (date).
The widow down by the brook:
a memoir of a time gone by / Mary MacNeill.
p. cm.
1. MacNeill, Mary (date). 2. MacNeill, Wilmot.
3. Country life—Connecticut—Canton Center.
4. Librarians—Connecticut—Hartford—Biography.
5. Prostate—Cancer—Patients—Biography.
6. Canton Center (Conn.)—Biography. I. Title.
F104.C2M33   1999
974.6'2—dc21
98-54771
CIP

ISBN 0-684-85969-6

*I dedicate this book to the memory of
my late husband, Wilmot "Mac" MacNeill, and
all the people of Canton Center, Connecticut, who
helped me through this time in my life.*

Acknowledgments

Special thanks to Kim Kanner, for her editorial support and immeasurable enthusiasm, and to Susan Moldow for her faith in my quiet, little story. Thank you to each member of the Scribner organization for creating the special package you have in your hands.

This book would not have been possible without the unique talent and appreciation of the Margret McBride Literary Agency, including Margret, Donna DeGutis, Jason Cabassi and, most of all, Kris Sauer. Without Kris's dedication, time and support, I would not have been able to complete this project. Thanks also to her mother, Salie Travis, for transferring my forty-five-year-old manuscript to disk.

The Widow
Down by the Brook

Author's Note

When people ask how I remembered all the things that happened, and all the people who worked on the house, I have to tell them about my awful habit of making notes. I always have thoughts about the smallest, everyday things running around in my head. So when there were a few minutes to spare and a few pieces of paper, I would write them down, often in letters to my friend Lil.

Lil said when she received one of my letters, she would phone some friends and put on a kettle for tea. They would sit around reading them, laughing and talking about our barn. Some time later, while her husband was away on business and Lil was staying at the house, she opened her purse and took out a package. She said she had saved all my letters, and told me I should put them all together in a story and call it *The Widow Down by the Brook*.

That was forty-six years ago, and that is how this story came to print.

I have been writer, editor, publisher, reviewer and librarian for all types of publications, and have self-published a few books. But this one never made it out of the box. There was always too much going on in my life to worry about getting it published.

Until now.

Prologue

Twenty miles west of the Hartford business district there is a haven of rural peace called Canton Center, population 440. We are three miles up from the Albany Turnpike. The air is free from traffic fumes and noise. The few autos that do come here are our own, friends', or those of delivery people from the city. The only sounds heard in the daytime are the singing of birds, the brook rippling over the rocks, trees rustling like a girl's taffeta skirt, the droning of bees in the wildflowers, the splash of a trout jumping after a fly.

At night, a plane flies over at nine o'clock. After that there is silence, emphasized, rather than broken, by the croaking of frogs, chirping crickets and katydids. Rabbits and woodchucks make their nocturnal search for food.

At dawn, the birds start greeting the new day. Squirrels race up and down the trees, saluting each other with their bushy tails, while their relatives, the chipmunks, romp in the garden. The rabbits, with their powder-puff tails bobbing, come to the back steps and brazenly lick whatever food is left in the cats' dish. The dogs chase each other around the woods. Day is here. Several minutes apart, three cars go down the road, and I know it is eight o'clock. Neighbors on their way to the city. Then the stillness is broken by the voices of children as they skip along the road to school.

The community consists mostly of farmers; two doctors and a few highly successful businessmen have estates out here. Up the road a piece there are three young families.

The Canton Center general store is the hub of activity. The post office occupies one end of it. It is open two hours in the morning and two in the afternoon. In the winter folks wait inside the store for the mail truck to arrive. The farmers talk about whose cow is about to freshen, or who is going to bring the cow for service. The businessmen talk about their deals. Most of the conversation takes place around the old potbellied black stove. The women gather in the corner by the window and talk about who's going to cook what for the church supper, who's going to bring what for the rummage sale.

Our address is RFD Collinsville. I could never figure out why. Collinsville is the next town over. We live in Canton Center. However, the confusion is more apparent than real. Mail seldom goes astray.

The scenery is varied and magnificent. When we leave the highway and ride up into the hills, the road becomes an avenue hedged by huge trees. Maples, oaks, elms and all the leaf trees form arches through which the sky is glimpsed colander-wise, a sky that is pale blue, trimmed with white puffs like ostrich feathers. In autumn, nature's paintbrush changes the appearance of the hills. They turn from shades of green to red, orange, gold, purple, pale yellow and sand color. Changes also occur in our methods of driving. Frequently, we have to stop our cars and yield right of way to a couple of deer, or a pheasant convoying her little ones across the road.

Then comes the beauty of winter. Snow covers the countryside. The brook tinkles prisms of ice with the touch of a musician. There is melody in the air of the sort which makes Jan Sebelius a celebrant of winter scenes. Add to this the merry voices of children, and the admonitory voices of their parents, as they skate over summer's swimming holes, and you have vividly in mind a picture of life in RFD Collinsville.

1

*H*ow will I tell him? How can I tell him?" Riding home that lovely autumn afternoon, I tried to dwell only on the spectacular beauty of the fall foliage. All the way out from West Hartford, over Avon Mountain, and along Albany Turnpike to Canton, the hills were carpeted with gold, red, brown and yellow leaves. The crisp ones blew and tapped on the windshield. I thought to myself, The leaves from the MacNeill family tree are beginning to swirl around me in the autumn of my life. Will I be able to rake them into a neat pile and start over?

The traffic was light at this time of day. People from the insurance companies were already home, and it was too early for the stores to close. The sky was steel gray, with the last rays of gold sifting through. Dawdling along at about thirty miles an hour, I was aroused from my depressing thoughts when three deer sprang out of the woods in front of the car and ran toward the brook. When we got to West Road, Inez stopped the car.

I couldn't go home yet. There was no easy way to tell him. How would he take it? What would I say? What would he say? He was a stalwart Scotsman, and I admired his strength. But a blow like this—even a Scotsman can only take so much. I thought I'd go the long way around, to give myself more time. Then I realized if I walked across the two rustic bridges, the noise of the loose, clanking boards would alert Smoky, and her barking would let Wilmot know I was there.

"You're late getting home," Wilmot said as I came in the back door. He was standing by the kitchen stove. "Sorry I didn't get the supper started." He kissed me, and held me a little longer than usual.

"I'll change my clothes, and we'll get it ready in a few minutes. What are we going to have?" It was difficult to control my voice. He fed Smoky and the cats, put some logs on the fire and lit the candles on the dining room table. We ate supper in a strained atmosphere of impending gloom, he wanting to ask, and me dreading to have to tell him.

After supper he lit his pipe and sat in the big leather chair by the fire. "Come sit down," he said. "We have to talk." He pushed out the ottoman for me to sit by his knees. "Did you call Dr. Wahro? I asked you to call, or go see him on your lunch hour."

I started to choke up, but managed a "Yes, I called him. Why can't we talk about it in the morning? Let's enjoy a nice evening by the fire."

"No. We have to talk about it now." He took my hand. "You have to tell me now. I must know. Don't you think it will be easier on both of us to know just where we stand?" He could feel my distress. He patted my hand. "Listen, dear, I know I haven't long to live. Come on now, how long? One month? Two months? Three months? I have to know."

"Dr. Wahro said he will drive out some day and have a talk with you."

"I have to know now. I can't wait for the doctor to come out." He relit his pipe. Then he put one hand under my chin and lifted my face up. As I looked straight into his eyes he said, "You know. So why can't I know?" He got up and paced the room. "You have to be brave and face it. You are not a child. In every couple one has to go first. In this instance, it's me. You will be left alone, and I know you will take care of yourself. You have a nice job. You will have a house of your own. You will get my army pension. Come now, tell me." He too was having a difficult time controlling his emotions.

I sobbed, "Three months."

We sat by the fire until after midnight. I brought him some wine. We talked about all the time he had spent looking for property—the farms he went to see—the real estate people and their aggressive ways, and the lovely, friendly country folks, who always had time to talk to a stranger and cheerfully give directions when you got lost up in the hills. By this time Smoky wanted to go out for a run. I let her out, and went to the cabinet to get Wilmot's medicine. I was wondering if the wine would have an effect on the drug, hoping that he would get some sleep. As I let Smoky in, Wilmot asked, "How long has it been since we did all the looking around, do you remember?"

"Yes," I said. "I remember."

2

*I*t was February 1951—one year ago—when he started looking for a place in the country. He went by himself those first
months. We were living in Somerville, Massachusetts, at the
time, and Wilmot was working at Pratt and Whitney Aircraft,
in East Hartford, Connecticut. Consequently, there was a lot
of commuting. He suggested that it would be better if we
moved to Connecticut, to save him the hours of travel and give
him more time to look at property.

I agreed to the move, and before long we rented a house in
East Hartford, on two acres of flat land; "good for the garden," he said. As soon as we were settled in our new environment I answered an ad in the *Hartford Courant* and got a job
as a librarian. It was pleasant working with books again. I had
Sundays and Mondays off, and could now go looking with
Wilmot.

For a while, everything went smoothly. Life was relatively
uneventful, as it is with most middle-aged couples. Our two

sons had long since embarked upon careers of their own. Bill, the older, was still in the navy. He had a wife, child and home in San Diego. Tom had also been in the navy, but only for four years. He was now working days as a photographer and attending college evenings.

Then suddenly, illness struck, and a series of cancer operations dictated Wilmot's early retirement. Prostate cancer is one of the more virulent types of the disease, and predictably incurable. Admittedly, this gloomy prognosis would have been enough to discourage the average man. But Wilmot was not average. He was an indomitable Scotsman, and his dream of owning a place in the country was indestructible. Together, we renewed our efforts to make his dream come true. To him, owning a piece of property with a brook running through it would be the height of success, the crowning achievement of his diminishing days. I realized, of course, that his ambition was far from selfish. But even in Connecticut, such dreams are difficult to translate into actuality. There were many places available, but only a few desirable. Availability and desirability, as is often the case, are greatly influenced by cost. We could only be as selective as our funds permitted.

We visited, corresponded with, telephoned and consulted an extraordinary number of real estate agents, each one of whom had intimate knowledge of the ideal place, a veritable heaven on earth. An agent in Simsbury showed us several and always with the recurrent phrase, "The television is good in this area." But he failed to say what else was good. TV reception must be a decisive factor in the choice of location for some clients. A broker in Granby was more resourceful, and reminded us that the surrounding hills afforded protection from atomic fallout. We went from one town to another, and after months of exhaustive, futile searching and outrageous prices, Wilmot decided to look at property out in the rural areas.

By June, we had seen a number of places, and one in particular ignited the torch of Wilmot's enthusiasm. It was situated in New Hartford, about twenty-five miles from Hartford. From a distance the scenic environment was eye-catching, but a closer look disclosed it as being marooned in the center of sixty-five acres of rocky, uneven land. The large cow barn had odoriferous evidence of its recent tenants. Large, yellow islands shone brazenly through the lime-coated floor, and the brilliant sun ridiculed rotted walls. A sagging roof threatened imminent collapse, and the floorboards were dangerously loose from the joists.

"This is a sportsman's paradise. Plenty of huntin' and fishin'," the real estate man told us. What he called a brook was a ditch about a foot wide filled with water running down from the hill. He continued, "Having water on the place is worth a thousand dollars, and electricity another thousand. Think of the money you won't have to spend. Can get a fellow to come in with a steam shovel and dig a swimming pool. It would only cost a few hundred dollars."

Frank and Mary Newmann, the first friends we had made since moving to Connecticut, were with us this Sunday. Wilmot and Frank remained unimpressed, but consented to continue with the inspection. Mary and I, being less venturesome, returned to the car, spread a blanket on a clear patch of grass, and prepared lunch. Mary looked at the men coming down through the property and said, "How can a person have such courage? Wilmot told Frank the other evening that there is nothing more that can be done for him, nothing now but painkillers." The sincerity of Mary's commiseration moved me deeply.

To conceal my own emotions I walked away toward the three men, who were back from the woods and leaning against an old wagon that had rusted outside the barn door. Wilmot came toward me reluctantly, his eyes half shuttered against the sun. He looked fatigued, but wouldn't admit it as he scratched a match across the seat of his pants and lit his pipe. His black, curly hair spiraled in the breeze. He was carelessly handsome.

Like many Scotsmen, he had twinkling blue eyes, was tall and well built, and wore his usual expression of complacency. Putting his arm around my shoulder, he inquired, "What do you want, dear?"

"You're not going to buy this place, are you?"

"What's the matter with it?"

"I don't think it's worth the price."

"Let me be the judge of that."

This was not the time or place to argue the point, so I returned to the car. A few minutes later I heard him say, "Thank you for your trouble. I'll let you know tomorrow." He and Frank joined us. The agent jumped into his jeep and dusted noisily up the road.

All the way home Wilmot talked to Frank about the improvements he planned. I sat there thinking, Improvements—there's nothing to improve. What could one do with a falling-down cow barn on the side of sixty-five hilly acres? Frank listened quietly, and after a while, he said, "What would you do with all that acreage? You couldn't work it, unless you wanted to start a quarry. You saw how rocky it is."

Wilmot was in no mood to be jocular and countered with a question of his own. "You saw all that pine on the hills, didn't you? There's lumber enough there to build a town. I could get it cut and seasoned. I'm a half-ass carpenter; I could do most of the work myself."

It was late afternoon when we returned to East Hartford. We dropped Mary and Frank off at their house and then went straight home. While I was cooking dinner, Wilmot sat at the kitchen table drawing plans. He was thinking aloud. "I'll put a picture window here, a fireplace there, and a large kitchen off the dining room."

I couldn't resist injecting an idea of my own. "Before you make any plans, dear, why don't you go over and talk to the carpenter on the next street. Ask him if he could go out with you tomorrow and see what he thinks of the place." Taciturnity being his forte, he mumbled an unintelligible reply and continued his sketching. Nevertheless, my suggestion bore results; shortly after dinner, I looked out the kitchen window and saw him crossing the back lawn toward the carpenter's house.

He soon returned and smilingly informed me, "He will come out with us in the morning."

All the way out to the property the men discussed the high prices of building material and labor. The real estate man was waiting for us. Soon, all three of them, ignoring my existence, began throwing specifications at each other with more enthusiasm than accuracy. As usual, differences of opinion were shouted, and concurrence whispered.

I remained in the car until the heat became insufferable, and I was forced to seek coolness in the barn. I heard my spouse briefing the agent: "Tell the owner I'll give him forty-two hundred for it." The agent nodded his head, waved good-bye to me and left. So did we, a short time afterward. The two men sat in the front seat, with me in the back on the way home.

The carpenter was a practical man who measured words and lumber with equal preciosity. "You asked for my opinion. I'm afraid you are not going to like it. That place would be a poor investment. You would be throwing money away. My advice is, look around some more." Wilmot didn't even bother to nod his head in acknowledgment of the counsel. He drove the rest of the way in lithic silence. The carpenter was silent too, and possibly regretted his frankness. After what seemed ages we were home again, and we let the carpenter off at his house.

Lunch was not enjoyable. Wilmot was still furious because his dream castle had been demolished by an expert. "The old bastard is jealous. I'll buy the place in spite of him." The bitter corollary that people who do things to spite others are busily chewing their own noses had momentarily escaped his attention.

"Shouldn't we look around some more?" I suggested mildly.

"I'm buying that place, and that settles it."

The drugs are changing his disposition, I thought to myself, and I won't say anything more.

3

I returned to work Tuesday morning, hoping that during the interim another client for the same property would outdistance us with a down payment. Fortune was definitely on my side. The agent telephoned Wilmot to report that the place had been sold for the listing price of $4,500.

The first greeting I got that night was "What did you tell the real estate man?"

"Nothing. What happened?"

"Well, the place has been sold. You must have told him that I wasn't working, and not to sell it to us."

"What difference would it make if you were working or not, if you had the money to buy the property?"

He looked so mortified, I felt sorry for him. He got up from the table and retired huffily to the den. His mortification was understandable. After all the months of diligent looking, he was convinced that he had found an answer to his dream, only to have it snatched away from him just when it seemed within his reach. I felt sorry for him, yet I was relieved he wasn't buying that particular place.

While doing the dishes, I heard the telephone ring. Wilmot answered it. He said, "Yes, nine o'clock Saturday morning will be all right."

I didn't ask questions, knowing that enlightenment would follow eventually. Saturday morning, he said he would drive me in town, because he was going to see some property out in Canton Center. That was the first mention of the call he had received Monday. It was a hot morning. He wore a sport shirt, open at the neck, and he looked cool and comfortable.

At six o'clock he was waiting for me at the corner of Morgan Street, beaming with news and optimism. He had found another dream castle in Canton Center, and he chattered happily about it all the way home.

"We'll go out and see it in the morning," he said, "and by God, we're going by ourselves this time."

Sunday morning at nine o'clock we started out for the country. Tom was also up early, packing and getting everything ready for a trip to Europe, Africa and Israel. His four years in the navy had been spent in the Pacific. He had taken hundreds of color slides. Now he wanted to augment his collection with pictures of the other side of the world.

It was literally cascading rain as we drove out to Canton Center. Finally we approached, with caution, the two rickety wooden bridges that spanned a wide brook. Then we came to a full stop. My intuition wasn't allowed to function, as Wilmot ecstatically proclaimed, "This is it!"

An abandoned clapboard barn confronted us from the midst of what appeared to be an impenetrable jungle. I asked, "How in the world do you get in there?"

"We got through the brush in a jeep yesterday. Hold on a minute, I'll cut a path." He took a sickle from the car trunk and advanced valiantly upon the weeds and bracken. I stumbled and grumbled behind him, protected from the rain and weeds by overshoes and heavy clothing, but the cold and dampness were penetrating.

This particular spot—this idyllic retreat from the city's turmoil—had three and a half acres of almost flat land bordering a brook, into which another, smaller brook somersaulted over mica-speckled rocks. There were three two-story buildings awaiting inspection, and several henhouses. The building near the road measured twenty-six by forty-two feet. The coach house attached to its north corner measured twenty-six by thirty-two feet. In the back, nearer to the brook, was a large red building. Wilmot also measured that one: it was thirty-eight by seventy feet. There had been water and electricity in the buildings a long time ago, but now the corroded pipes protruded like so many petrified snakes, and the greenish, naked wiring looped dejectedly from the ceiling and beams.

The barn near the road had concrete floors under the cow stalls, and the cedar four-by-fours that separated them had been scalloped by generations of restive cows. The back of the barn was like a city dump. A low concrete wall paralleled its entire length. Wilmot referred to it as a "pig run." The right side of the structure was crammed with so much junk he had to struggle with the door. Everything that was conceivably of use to a farmer had been stored through the years. Numerous hens' nests were nailed against the left wall, and there were also rabbit hutches and turkey pens. We climbed the ladder to the second floor and found more nests, and shelflike dropboards on which the accumulated manure was at least six inches thick. The entire wooden floor was also thick with manure. The hayloft was full of dry, dusty hay guarded by truculent wasps.

When our interior inspection ended, we went outside and viewed the coach house. The first floor of that dilapidated structure was also full of junk: an old divan, burned at one end; a refrigerator with the motor removed; and an antique wardrobe bulging with canning jars, stone jugs, whisky bottles and old dishes. The second floor was even less inviting. We then went outside, and Wilmot paced off the distance from the buildings near the road to the red building. He said it was roughly three hundred feet. We went inside for a second look. Although partitioned into rooms, it had been used exclusively for hens. The laying charts were nailed up all over the walls. The roof was leaking badly, and the rain made the floor, covered with manure, dangerously slippery, and the odor nauseating. We hastened back to the barn. Wilmot measured it again and gleefully reiterated, "This will make a good-sized house. Yes, sir, twenty-six by forty-two."

"How would I get to work from out here?"

"How does anyone else get to work?" He walked over and looked out the back door. "My mind is made up," he said in a serious, almost solemn voice. "I'm buying this place."

I'm buying this place. The words hit me like a blow in the stomach. Buying a place twenty miles northwest of Hartford, and having to drive over Avon Mountain to get to it. It was a place with not a house in sight, no one around. He knew how serious his condition was. He said repeatedly, "My time is running out. I must get you settled in a home of your own before I kick the bucket." His strength of character was all that kept him going.

"Let's sit in the car and get warm," I managed to say. I poured his hot coffee from the thermos and the boiling water from another bottle for my tea. We ate lunch without much conversation. I remarked, "Here it is July. We have a holiday coming up." No response. He was thinking.

We went back to the barn. He took the sickle and laboriously cut a narrow path to the brook. It was unquestionably picturesque through the veils of rain. The overhanging trees washed their branches in the translucent water, and an occasional trout surfaced abruptly for unwary flies. Wilmot was silently admiring the scene, and seemed momentarily overcome by nostalgic memories.

"Look at that trout," he exclaimed. "It must be twelve

inches. Did you ever see such a beautiful brook? It's about twenty feet wide." Then he pointed to the various trees individually, reciting their names with a readiness born of long acquaintanceship. Leaving the brook reluctantly, he set out to look for the well. "It should be somewhere near the barn," he said as he swung the sickle. Soon he hit a pile of rocks. He pulled some weeds by hand, then I heard, "I found the well. Look at that sparkling water. No stagnancy here. This well is spring fed." He was delighted to have pure drinking water available.

On the way back from the well, we discovered the blackened foundation of a burned house and some charred lumber. We went inside the coach house. Wilmot lit his pipe and pulled up an old box to serve as a seat. He referred to the advantages of owning a farm. We could, he said, buy a cow, a couple of pigs, some hens and have a garden. Living should then be economical. He made no reference, of course, to the arduous, dawn-to-dusk work on which such economy is founded. Through the open doorway we could see grapevines climbing the maple trees, and moribund apple trees entwined by wild raspberries.

Suddenly, looking through the mess of foliage, I caught a glimpse of a chimney, and what looked like part of a white house . . . or was it a white cloud appearing in the sky?

I said to Wilmot, "Look up there. Do you think there is a house? Let's drive up the road. If there is someone around, you could ask about the brook. It probably floods every year."

He decided to humor me, and we drove up the road a short distance and saw a wide blacktop driveway with a two-car garage near the road. We went up the driveway and saw a two-story white farmhouse. A petite, vivacious young woman answered Wilmot's door knuckling, and a huge Saint Bernard stood within nuzzling distance of her hand. We introduced ourselves, told her the purpose of our visit, and she smilingly invited us inside. She listened to our queries attentively, and then summoned her husband, who was painting screens in the basement. He was a tall, young man, pleasant-looking, quiet voiced and, at the same time, keenly alert and businesslike. Both men soon withdrew to a side porch, opened cans of beer and engaged in amiable discussion about things in general. Mrs. Ferguson and I remained in the kitchen. She made a pot of tea, and brought some cookies from the pantry. She told me about several of her friends who had bought barns and converted them into charming homes.

Later we joined our husbands on the porch. Wilmot was saying, "I'm going to buy that place. Do you know of a good lawyer out here who would handle such a small transaction?"

"Well, I'll be damned," exclaimed Mr. Ferguson. "I'm a lawyer, and would be glad to take care of the closing for you. What's more, I've had the whole parcel surveyed and maps made in the hope of adding it to my present property. The owner died and his widow sold the farm in several parcels. It was a big piece of property, on both sides of the road. The old farmhouse burned, I'm told. A doctor up the road bought fifteen acres. A fellow across from here, in the woods, bought twenty-two acres. A family from West Hartford bought fifteen acres in the woods, almost across from the bridges. They plan on building this summer."

I interrupted, "Did you ask Mr. Ferguson about the brook, dear? Does it flood in the spring?"

Without waiting for Wilmot to relay the question, the lawyer replied, "We've been out here a year now, and I haven't seen it flood." His answer was wonderfully reassuring, and helped dispel any doubts about the prospective purchase.

Mrs. Ferguson told us about the congenial neighbors we would have, and about the social affairs held frequently at the community house down in the center: strawberry festivals, church suppers, square dances and open-air plays.

It was late afternoon when we started for home. Wilmot was in a jubilant mood, and hummed a Scottish ballad with considerable verve and trueness of pitch. We stopped off at the Newmanns' to tell them about the property in Canton

Center and Wilmot's end of the search. Both Mary and Frank were glad that he hadn't bought the place in New Hartford.

Mary said she saw bats hanging from the rafters. "I saw them too," I replied, "but I thought they were birds."

Wilmot shook with laughter and said, "A hell of a farmer you'll make."

4

$\mathcal{M}$onday morning, July 2. The house was as clamorous as a Mexican bazaar, with everyone trying to perform two or more things at once. Tom had finished his packing. He was excited about his trip and didn't eat much breakfast. Wilmot wanted me to pack a lunch. He was planning to stay all day at the barn. I was trying to make the beds and do a little tidying up. It was, no doubt, a fairly representative scene of domestic disorder, not wholly divested of a certain degree of down-to-earthness.

We dropped Tom off at the bus depot in Hartford. It seemed strange saying good-bye to him again; he had been home for such a short time. Like most young veterans he found readjustment to civilian life frustrating. He couldn't relax or settle down. From the bus depot we went to the bank. Wilmot wanted to have some money transferred from his savings to his checking account to pay for the building materials and tools. "Instant money," he called it.

We did more weeding, more measuring, more cussing and some calculating.

"I'll make a two-story colonial house out of the barn," he said.

"Why don't you work on the long red building now? That could be converted to a beautiful ranch house."

"No, the two-story house is more practical for our present circumstances. Besides, the barn is more conveniently situated. It is near the road, water and power lines. I know what I'm doing, dear."

My objection invalidated, I began to prepare lunch. The fresh air and arduous labor had honed our appetites to razor sharpness. We lunched with more celerity than constraint. When things were put away and we sat on the step of the barn, just looking toward the road, Wilmot said, "Don't worry about Tom. All the kids go through hell when they come home from the service. Their friends are away, or in some cases they have lost their pals. They are home and have no one to go places with. I know. I went through it after World War One. I traveled everywhere before I got settled. It takes time."

He then suggested that we stop at the Hartford *Times* office on the way home and look through their books of house plans.

Wednesday, the Fourth of July, the library was closed. Wilmot called me for breakfast at six o'clock. I arose yawning regretful farewells to slumber, and ate my tea, toast and marmalade. He cooked himself the usual bacon and eggs. As soon as we finished eating, we packed the car icebox and were en route to the country. We wore heavy clothes to guard against the sting nettles and wild raspberry vines. It was still early when we got there. Serenity was all about us, and Tennyson's tireless brook was babbling.

I chatter, chatter as I flow
To join the brimming river,

> *For men may come and men may go*
> *But I go on forever.*

At that moment, the prospect of prolonged physical exertion was more perturbing than pleasing, more inhibiting than challenging.

Wilmot had bought a large scythe for himself and a small one for me. Together we cut through the weeds until lunchtime. Boxes from the coach house served as chairs, and while the steak broiled on the new charcoal burner, he cleaned off a rabbit hutch, spread some newspapers on it and improvised a table. Tomatoes and lettuce from the little icebox were cool and crisp. It was truly a delectable meal. The resumption of work was now less repellent. By heaping the leaves and weeds into a neat pile, we soon had a clear patch behind the barn, as well as a path all around it. Time seems to quicken in its passage when we take no note of it, or maybe the aperture in the inverted hourglass suddenly widens, and the old man's sickle drops a little closer to our necks.

The rest of the week Wilmot went out to the country alone. He accomplished quite a lot by himself. He removed the hens' nests and dropboards from the walls downstairs, and added all that to the pile of debris, which was becoming mountainous. It was a worry having him in the woods alone. I suggested that he put some of his prescription in a little bottle and keep it in the glove compartment. He was, however, frank to admit he missed me, and looked forward to our weekend collaboration.

On Sunday, July 8, we were teammates again. It was an unbearably hot day. With a wrecking bar borrowed from Mr. Ferguson, Wilmot assaulted the inside walls on the first floor. Some of the wood was rotted and had to be discarded immediately. Whatever was good he salvaged, and he taught me how to pull the nails out without bending them. When this became too warm a job, I went outside and started the lunch. During the week Wilmot had spread sand on a cleared space outside the back door and built an open fire ring. It had the rack from the old refrigerator on top of it to hold the pots. There were plenty of small pieces of wood to burn, and that was quicker than the charcoal. The aroma of chops and vegetables cooking was appetizing, and the little woods animals showed their interest with twitching noses and daring proximity. One chipmunk sat on a nearby rock soliciting tidbits, as a squirrel clamored excitedly for a share.

After the dishes had been washed and put away, we strolled down to the brook and sat for a few minutes watching a chipmunk patiently training her little ones in the art of rock jumping. When they slipped off the rocks into the water, she would nose them back up and start over. We left quietly without disturbing the exercise.

We had a little portable with us at the barn. The weatherman predicted that the hot weather would be with us all week. That was not good news for hardworking people. The afternoon chore was even more repugnant. Wilmot asked me to remove a pile of manure from near the back of the barn to a spot over near the edge of the cleared land. "I've cut a path for the wheelbarrow," he said, "to make the job easier." In no time at all, I appeared doomed to a permanent crouch. My sporadic efforts to straighten up during the wheelbarrowing must have been conspicuous, for there was a note of compassion in my helpmate's voice when he said, "Come over here, I have an easier job for you. Move this pile of wood. Throw it through the coach house window."

"What do you want to move it for?"

"To make a place for the new lumber I ordered."

"Why don't we sit down for a few minutes. I'll make some tea."

"We didn't come out here to have a picnic." He stomped away, radiating disapproval.

I realized from this attitude that his suffering was becoming unbearable, and I knew he would never give up. I went out to the car and brought in his pills.

5

*A*nother Monday. Another day off at the library. The temperature was still in the nineties, and I was back at my job in the woodpile. As I picked up the pieces and tossed them through the coach house window, a large, black snake with a white belly slithered out from the side of the pile. Too tired and warm to bother running from it, I threw a piece of wood at it. It reared up, hissed defiance and disappeared into its nest. "Stay there, you slimy thing, and don't bother me."

Wilmot overheard the one-sided conversation and came quickly to my side. "What's the matter, getting hysterical or something?"

"There's a big, black snake here. It went back in the corner."

He picked up his old straw hat and passed it to me. "Put this on your head; you've been out in the sun too long."

"You don't believe me."

"It isn't a question of belief. Some people are affected by long exposure to the sun. Sit down awhile."

While I was having my little rest, Wilmot dug through another pile of rubbish. He unearthed an old bedspring made of wooden laths. He wiped off the dirt and put some feedbags on it. Then he went out to the car and got the two old blankets he used to keep the tools from rattling and spread them on top of the bags. He carefully moved his "bed" to the side of the room, lit his pipe and reclined.

The day passed without further incidents, and we were pleased with ourselves, the world and, most of all, with the transformation taking place around us.

Tuesday's lunch hour was spent buying assorted tools at the nearby Sears & Roebuck, a most unusual deviation from the routine of resting and relaxing on the cathedral patio. It is definitely good for one's soul to devote a few minutes each day to contemplation, in or out of church. For different people, there are different places and different ways to achieve such an end. A short poem by a friend seems to support that viewpoint.

> *I like to watch the shadows cast*
> *A net of dusk along the sea,*
> *And hear the small waves trolling prayers*
> *Upon their pebbled rosary.*
>
> *My church is then a sandy cove*
> *Its lofty dome the sky*
> *And for an altar I accept*
> *The proud moon riding high.*

The hot weather persisted, but it did not interfere with Wilmot's daily work at the barn. When he stayed until late afternoon, he picked me up at six o'clock. He loved to discuss in detail the progress he was making. Hard as I worked, there wasn't the slightest doubt that he was working harder, and I realized fully that he was doing it all for me.

When he finished telling me about his work, he would ask, "How did it go in the library today?"

I would tell him about the different customers. They were getting more difficult in the hot weather, and more impatient. No one wanted to wait to be checked out. They would start to walk out with the books under their arms, saying, "Put it on my card." The library was humid, with only the electric fans stirring up the hot air.

One woman asked for a book with *inter* in the title. She said, "I know it isn't *intercourse,* but I do know that it has *inter* in it." I took a copy of *Intermission,* a story about the theater, off the shelf and checked it out for her. Another woman asked for the new mystery by Churchill. She said, "I know I didn't see any other mysteries by him. He must be a new writer." I had to think on that one. Then I passed her a copy of Sir Winston Churchill's new book, *Hinge of Fate.* She returned it the next day, saying, "That ain't a mystery."

It was hard to keep a straight face, especially in these cases, like the woman who asked for a good, spicy book called *I Took It Lying Down.* I did tell her the difference. I said, "Mrs. Jones, that is not a spicy book, it is the story of a girl in a TB sanatorium."

"I thought it was something for my husband." She smiled.

All the chatter about customers kept him laughing, and we would be home in a short time, get supper and help him relax.

Sunday, July 22. My birthday. A minimum of housecleaning had to be done before we took off for the woods. Wilmot hadn't the vaguest appreciation of that fact as he rushed around fussing, tutting, shaking his head, mumbling. "What in the hell keeps a woman so long?"

Finally, the car was loaded and we were driving out Route 44 in Hartford, when I remembered something. "Did you bring the aluminum pot to boil water for our tea?"

"No," he replied without hesitation.

"Let's go back and get it."

"We won't go back for anything. You already spent half the day getting ready."

We drove for miles in silence. Then, as we turned up West Road, he stopped by a dairy farm, looked out the car window and exclaimed, "Did you ever see anything so beautiful?" The cows grazed placidly in the pasture. The birds circled against the clear, blue sky. The roadside was covered with wildflowers in full bloom. It was beautiful.

Then the scene changed abruptly as the barn came into view. There was more assorted rubbish outside, giving towering evidence of the progress he had made during this week. It looked a lot different inside, almost skeletal. The entire floor had been ripped up. He had a fellow come and chop up the concrete floor and toss all that outside, while he had pulled up the wooden part of the flooring. He took my hand as we walked cautiously on the twelve-inch beams spanning the cellar hole. A serious injury or broken bones would be the consequence of a single misstep; a fall to the cellar would be seven feet. The rest of the building had a crawl space of two feet. It was then that I began to appreciate the full magnitude of our undertaking, the enormous amount of backbreaking, costly labor that lay between us and the day the house would be finished. Was it fortitude or stubbornness that gave him the will to continue? At any rate, he devoted little time to reverie. He was already pulling three- and four-inch nails from the salvaged boards. For a few minutes he seemed unaware of my meditative immobility. I stood there staring at the gaping hole in the ceiling until he demanded, with considerable asperity, "What's keeping you?"

"The stairs are gone. How do I get up?" My job for the day was to clean the manure off the floor upstairs.

"I have a little ladder for you." He shouldered an old ladder and carried it outside, placing it directly under one of the upstairs windows. Like a captain ordering a sailor to the lookout, he said, "Climb up there."

I climbed upward with more temper than timidity, but was

unable to get from the top rung in through the window. My clumsiness exasperated him. "Grab the sill and pull yourself up," he hollered and walked away unconcernedly.

I renewed my efforts, trying at the same time to ignore the innumerable wasps swarming in the sun. I didn't admit that I was afraid of them. Wilmot despised cowardice as much as ineptitude. Finally, with supreme effort and some skin-scraping, I managed to half scramble, half fall inside.

Using a square-edged shovel, I attacked the floor with the ferocity of a Dutch housewife, but without much success. Then I got down on my knees, wielding a putty knife and trowel. The hen manure was as hard as cement. It would take a lifetime to scrape away the twenty-six by forty-two feet of obdurate matter. I called to Wilmot and asked him to bring me some water. Obligingly, he freed a partially covered milk can from the rubbish heap, set it in the wheelbarrow and trundled up to the well. All the way back, the water slopped over him at every bump, and he was wetter and madder than a wet hen. Ill temper intensified his taciturnity. He transferred some of the water to an old bucket and carried it up the ladder. He also passed up an old broom and a bottle of barcolene.

I sprinkled a large area, and the manure softened. I swept and shoveled until my hands blistered. When the water was used up, and the wet section looked like mud with little patches of wooden floor showing through, I filled the bucket with the manure, carried it over, and dumped it out the window. Unfortunately, Wilmot had picked that spot to sit on a nail barrel and have a few relaxing minutes smoking his pipe. I looked out to see what all the cursing was about. There he stood, covered from head to waist in manure. He hollered, "I've often been told I was full of shit—and now I am."

As he walked toward the brook he looked back and hollered, "Don't put any more shit in that bucket. I have to put it down the well." Before long I heard a splash. By the time I climbed down the ladder, he reappeared, hurting and swearing. "That damn turtle I stepped on looked like a rock." He changed into some dry things. Even in the ninety-degree weather, he worked fully clothed. He said clothes prevented sunburn.

He took a pill, and some coffee from his thermos. He quieted down in a short time, and I climbed back upstairs. It was sweltering, and the perspiration wasps were hovering around me. These insects sting people to get the salt from their perspiration. Before long, Wilmot called, "Lunch."

"Come and help me get down."

"Put your arse on the edge of the window, and get down the way you got up."

"The wasps and bees are all around me. I don't want to get stung."

He came to the ladder and helped me down, saying, "Aren't you ever going to learn how to take care of yourself?" There was that phrase again. I realized by now that he wasn't being callous. He was just trying to make me independent.

He had borrowed a bucket from the Fergusons' barn and boiled water to make the tea. In spite of the morning's tribulations, we enjoyed our lunch, although I drank only one cup of tea instead of the usual two or three. Squeamishness had inhibited my thirst. Sometimes a too vivid imagination is far from being an asset. In time I learned to accept the fact that temporary hardships give the ordinary comforts of life the appearance of luxury. Perhaps that is why Wilmot's improvised bed was so utterly satisfying whenever exhaustion and pain forced him to rest. He rarely complained. His philosophy was, Do what you can, as well as you can, but do it. He combined the unique qualities of stoic and pragmatist without sacrificing his innate kindness and his recognition of the spiritual side of life.

He was in excellent humor after his rest, and he smiled as he filled the bucket from the water in the milk can and passed it to me to tote upstairs. Continuous scraping and scrubbing began to show results. Now most of the floor was clean and sweet smelling. As I needed more water, he refilled the bucket.

The barcolene ate holes in my rubber gloves and my hands were smarting, but the sense of achievement was a potent anodyne.

Wilmot too was making progress. The stringers were all down for the subflooring. From a stack of salvaged boards, he sawed pieces into various lengths and showed me how to nail them in place. I soon learned how to use a hammer. We toiled until dark, and then sat by the fire watching the moon etch the trees against the sky. Those precious moments of serenity and silence still enrich my storehouse of memories.

6

*T*he next weekend, cooking outdoors was a lot easier. During the week Wilmot had constructed a fireplace from concrete blocks and iron gratings he discovered up by the old, burned foundation. This new facility was safer in two ways: The pots and pans couldn't tip over, and if a piece of burning wood dropped out, it just smoldered on the dry sand.

The sweltering weather continued, and inside the barn the wasps continued their defiance of frequent spraying. No doubt they were determined that interlopers from the city's concrete pastures should be subjected to constant harassment.

The barn was slowly becoming more homelike. The living room had subflooring down and extra joists installed where needed. That sort of work could be done single-handedly, but Wilmot needed my aid for heavier undertakings. This was ponderously true when he decided to remove one of the eight-by-eight chestnut beams in the wall to make an opening for a door from the living room to the front hall. First we had to place four-by-fours to support the ceiling. When that was done, he tied a rope around the beam and told me to steady it while he sawed through it. That considerable feat exhausted us both. He looked tired and sick. I suggested he rest for a few minutes, and I would bring him a glass of milk.

On the way back in from the car icebox, I heard a crashing, splintering noise, then the hollering and swearing. Wilmot was walking across the twelve-by-twelve joists over the cellars when he lost his footing and fell. He was suspended there, his face on one joist, and a leg caught up over the other. He was crying out in pain and couldn't move. I couldn't reach high enough to free him. I ran back down to the cellar to get the old rabbit hutch to stand on. I lifted his leg as gently as possible, then tried to hold him by the hips to help him down to the cellar floor. He clung to me as we came up the cellar steps.

"What were you doing?" I asked timidly.

In a trembling voice, he answered, "I was walking across to the other side to get the goddamn tobacco. I wanted to fill my pipe."

"Lie down a little while," I suggested, "the water is boiling. I'll make some tea."

"Let's get going," he said. "I have a house to build."

"Can I get your pills or something?" I asked, wondering how a man can be so determined. Scotsmen certainly are a hardy race. They do not nurse their bruises, they berate and ignore them.

"Get the needle out of the glove compartment and give me a shot." The doctor had instructed me how to administer the morphine. In the past few weeks I took it with us.

The drug relieved the pain, and he went back to work. I nailed down some boards for the subflooring over the cellar. If that part of the flooring was down, we would be able to walk around more freely. But Wilmot was exhausted from the fall, and reluctantly put away his tools. He let me drive home.

After supper, he went to bed with an ice bag on his face, a hot water bottle under his back and more medication.

As usual, on Tuesdays, my regular customers would ask

about our activities on the weekend. I felt sure they doubted a lot of the things I told them. They did not mean to challenge my veracity, they were simply incredulous. One woman said to me, "You look so sophisticated and ladylike. I can't imagine you doing a man's work out there in the woods." Men were less dubious, and would jokingly ask advice concerning problems in carpentry.

During the week my lunch hours were spent shopping for more tools. I bought an electric saw, but the store didn't have an extra blade. Wilmot wanted a rip guide, and also a crosscut blade. By Saturday, the store manager had the rip guide for me.

It was now the fifth of August. We were at the barn at 7:30 A.M. to finish the subflooring. I could hardly believe it. There it was, 1,092 square feet of salvaged lumber, fitted, sawed and nailed—and above all, safe to walk on. Every bit of the floor was covered, except the opening for the fireplace.

During the week, Wilmot had gone shopping in the village of Collinsville and bought a pump to draw the water from the well. He soon learned that tradesmen in the country worked when they felt like it, and not when you needed them. I carried water from the brook. That was easier for me than lowering the bucket down in the well and pulling it up full. We had the electric saw, and no electricity; the pump, and no water.

Wilmot decided to go upstairs and remove the hay from the hayloft. In spite of the heat and humidity, he thought it would be safer to have the dry hay removed. He said it was a fire hazard. Forkful after forkful of dry, dusty hay was tossed out one of the front windows. He said he could not let any hay fly around near the open fire in the back of the barn. The wasp's nests were being thrown out with the hay. The insects resented their eviction, and flew back through the window, revenge-bound. They swarmed around him and crawled up the legs of his pants. He was stung in many places but bore the pain stoically, and would not come down. He told me to make mud packs and bring them up. We moved to the other side of the attic, and the application of the mud eased the pain. I shall never cease to wonder at the capacity of human beings to endure acute physical discomfort when they are resolved to pursue a certain course of action.

The next morning the men from the electric company installed a power line. It lit and lightened our labors at the same time. Wilmot whistled as he sawed studs for partitions. The lumber was a conglomerate of cherry and cedar posts that were originally the cow stalls. They were tough, seasoned and completely free from wormholes and dry rot. No better material could be purchased at any price. As the partitions rose, one by one, Wilmot was delighted with his plan of room arrangement. A large living room was his first objective. Its dimensions would be eighteen by twenty-six, with the five-foot-wide fireplace, bricked to the ceiling and flanked by bookcases. Next would come the bedrooms, dining room, kitchen and bath. The second-floor bedrooms and bath would come later.

Going home along the winding country roads, now fragrant with new-mown hay, he divulged his plans for the coming week. "Tomorrow morning, I'm going to take one of the twin beds from the attic with me, some bedclothes and shaving gear and stay until Saturday afternoon." He planned to pick me up after work on Saturday. I would go with him Sunday morning, and we would return home Monday night.

I asked, "Won't you be nervous in the woods at night, in a place with no doors or windows?"

"You don't need to lock yourself in when you live in the country. There is far more danger from intruders in the city." His mind was made up. He changed the subject. "You haven't told me anything about your customers lately."

"Miss Marsh came in Friday. As usual, she wanted a minister, or divorce story. She said, 'I just love divorces. I wish I could get married so as I could get a divorce.' I gave her one of Faith Baldwin's light romances. Another customer asked for *Florence Nightgown*. I gave her a copy of *Florence Nightin-*

gale. She went away smiling, 'Thank you, dear, that will hold me for tonight.' Another one said, 'I'd like something pleasant when I go to bed tonight.' I gave her the new Elizabeth Seifort book."

All the chatter about customers kept him laughing, and we were home in a short time. He went to bed right after supper, but awoke at nine o'clock. He was in great pain and needed a shot.

Tuesday morning while I was getting breakfast ready, he loaded the top of the car, as well as the inside of it, with all his essentials for light housekeeping. He dropped me off in Hartford, and drove off as happy as a kid going on a camping trip.

Mary Newmann met me in town for lunch. She was surprised when I told her about Wilmot going to stay in the country all week. She said, "He's crazy. Suppose he runs out of medicine, or if he gets worse and needs a shot. He can't do that himself."

I said, "Mrs. Ferguson said she would keep an eye on him. She will send the boys down to see how things are going. She also said there is a doctor up the road. He doesn't have an office in his house, he works in Hartford. But in case of an emergency, she was sure he would attend to things—that is, if he were home."

Mary asked, "Couldn't you talk him out of it?"

"I have learned that when his mind is made up, dynamite could not change it," I told her.

The next Monday we made a trip to the lumber company. It took two hours to choose the doors, windows, trim and hardware. Wilmot also ordered a thousand feet of number-one select oak flooring for the living room. Parting with so much money in a lump sum is a melancholy experience for those who have more cents than dollars.

It was a beautiful day. We were back at the barn by eleven o'clock. I put on some vegetables as soon as the fire was started. The outdoor fireplace was still intact. Only two pieces of concrete has fissioned so far, but it remained upright and serviceable. After lunch, Wilmot took a rest and I walked down to the brook. Mirrorlike, it mimed its surroundings with matchless artistry. The sky was intensely blue, with fleecy white clouds. The chipmunks scurried about the rocks, and squirrels skittered up and down the trees.

The next week was the beginning of my long-awaited vacation. We were up at six o'clock. Wilmot carried down the other twin bed and roped it to the top of the car. Trunk and backseat were filled with groceries, household items, clothes, toilet articles and the little icebox. Milk and eggs we could buy from the farmer up the road, and bread and daily necessities were available at the Canton Center store. Loading the car took longer than usual because of the rain. This morning Wilmot had to carry everything into the garage, then decide where to put what. Other times he could drive up to the back door. But even the heavy rain had failed to dampen his spirits.

It stopped by the time we arrived at the barn, but pools of water were everywhere, and ankle-deep mud did its best to make us step out of our shoes. We had long since grown inured to nature's pranks, and managed to retain both shoes and sanity. Wilmot whistled lightheartedly as he unloaded the car.

In the back-bedroom part of the barn, we now had twin beds, a big old milk table he moved up from the red building, an old rattan chair and a Boston rocker. The place was rapidly becoming more homelike, in a primitive sort of way. While I was washing the big, sturdy table, I asked Wilmot, "Why do you call this a milk table? What was it used for?"

He said, "Dairy farmers put a large, heavy table, strong enough to hold hundreds of pounds of milk, in cans, out near the road. That makes it more convenient for the truck driver when he stops to collect the milk."

"How did you get that up to the barn by yourself?"

"I put it across the wheelbarrow."

"Do the farmers milk cows at the same time every day?" I asked.

"Twice a day," he replied, "at five o'clock in the morning

and at five in the afternoon. And they don't work on daylight savings time. If a man wants to go away on a Sunday, he has to arrange for someone to come and milk his cows. That's a farmer's life. Seven days a week. Every day of the year." While he was talking, he kept busy building a shelf for his medicine, pipe, tobacco and matches.

There were times when morbid speculations haunted my nights. He was suffering more these days. I asked myself if he would live to see his dream castle grounded on solid earth. At such times, a poem ran through my head.

> When I was full of childish fun
> I built a castle free of stone,
> Such beauty graced it that the sun
> Agreed to shine on it alone.
> But since I learned to fret and frown,
> As older folks so often do,
> My castle tall has toppled down,
> The sun has grown indiff'rent too.

The similarity between a castle and a barn undergoing the metamorphosis into a home is not as fanciful as it seems. After all, a man's home is his castle, and I was obviously the chatelaine. Unquestionably, that too was Wilmot's attitude. Like all fiercely independent men, he had little love for the modern cave dwelling that one finds in huge apartment buildings in the city. He wanted a place of his own, no matter how modest, from which he could step outside and breathe the fresh air, and walk on earth firm enough to support his weight, and fruitful enough to provide sustenance for living.

Housekeeping out-of-doors had several advantages. There were no floors to wash and wax, no rugs to vacuum and no windows to clean. Water for cooking and washing was carried from the brook and stored in the rain barrel at the corner of the barn. Utensils for the preparation of food were few and versatile. After meals the silver was washed and stored in a bread box. Dishes were washed and stacked on the old table and covered with a plastic tablecloth to protect them from dust and flies. The pans were hung on nails and the dish towels washed and hung on the rungs of the ladder, which now rested against an apple tree. The fire was kept alive all day with heavy pieces of logs. There was always boiling water for tea.

Wilmot awoke from his nap, and he went to the living-room part of the barn to try to assemble a "ready-to-assemble" window. He was not immediately successful. This irked him tremendously, as he sat on his nail-barrel chair extemporizing some colorful abuse for those precut windows intended to be put together by an amateur. It was earthy without being vulgar.

Night finally put an end to our minor tribulations. We retired to the comparative comfort of our doorless, window-less, cool barn—now furnished with the luxury of electricity. An extension cord draped from a beam over the beds supported a miniature moon of 100 watts. It helped me forget the bats, which occasionally darted in and out through the open spaces, but it attracted the flies and mosquitoes. There was no way to curb their trespassing.

I turned off the light, but sleep would not come. I did not wish to awaken Wilmot, so I pulled the sheet over my head and tried to read by flashlight. It didn't work. Then I assumed a kneeling position, with the book on the pillow, and the sheet poked rumpwise. That too was unsatisfactory. There is no substitute for sleep. Meanwhile, I remembered being told that bats get into women's hair. So I got up and tied a scarf about my head, and then went back to bed, hoping for better results. It was futile; I was not even drowsy. It was now after midnight, and a heavy workday faced us. The mason and his helpers were coming to build the fireplace and chimney. I reminded myself, I must get some rest.

That was all I remembered until Wilmot called to me. He was in pain and needed something. It was two o'clock. I had a thermos of boiling water ready for such emergencies. Hot tea and the pill relaxed him, and he dozed. I went back to bed. He called me again at six o'clock. He needed more medicine. The longest span between pills now was three to four hours. We stayed up. It was a beautiful morning, still cool, the birds singing and the brook sparkling in the sun.

Poets say nothing is as quickly forgotten as the night before. They must mean the striking difference between darkness and light, the sorrow of yesterday and the hope for tomorrow.

7

A fireplace is somewhat like a giraffe. The hearth is its stomach and the long, tapering chimney, not too unlike a neck, channels its smoky breath into the sky. That is, no doubt, a fanciful notion, but there is nothing imaginary about the hard work which makes a fireplace possible. Two thousand five hundred used bricks were piled near the back of the barn awaiting the arrival of the workmen. The mason was a capable man who knew what to do, and wasted no time doing it.

After a brusque hello, he said, "I need two yards of sand right away. You can order it from Collinsville." I thought to myself, He must be crazy—two yards of sand? I drove up and told Mrs. Ferguson what the mason needed. She phoned in the order. We chatted a few minutes, and then I returned to the brick pile. Wilmot had overlooked the fact that the bricks didn't hold themselves together. The mason was impatient. "I can't use them bricks till you clean the mortar off 'em." He looked at me. "Get a putty knife, and I'll show you how to clean 'em."

While he demonstrated the art of cleaning the bricks, he gave me further instructions about their disposition. Evidently, I had been chosen as his number-two helper. I didn't object. My participation in the undertaking would help lower the cost. Tradesmen in the country were paid by the hour, not the job. The bricks had to be sorted into five categories: colored, broken, good, chipped and fragmentary. So, I would have to arrange them in separate piles.

The sun was scorching hot, and the humidity suffocating—a typical August dog day. I put on a shirt to protect my arms and shoulders. The mosquitoes, immune to all our sprays, were making it more miserable. It was difficult to work with canvas gloves on, but without them my hands would bleed. As I cleaned the bricks, the number-one helper carried them to his boss. There was a minimum of talking and a maximum of endeavor. Before we realized it, lunchtime was upon us.

I doffed gloves and went in to see what Wilmot wanted to eat. To my surprise he was lying on the bed. I knew instantly that he was having one of his bad spells, now more frequent, and of longer duration. He would not, I knew, welcome the least hint of sympathy. Maintaining my equanimity with some effort, I asked, "What would you like for lunch, dear?"

"Give me some hot soup and tea."

The meal was easily prepared, and would no doubt have been consumed quickly as on other occasions had not the mason, an outspoken man, chosen that moment to make what he mistakenly considered a hilarious remark: "It's funny, you know, the first time I saw youse people here, I thought youse were tramps."

Wilmot turned livid, and gave every indication of a man about to blow his stack. He stood up abruptly and hurried outside. I joined him a few minutes later, my mission one of pacification. I said, "We probably did look like tramps to anyone passing by. Come back and finish your lunch. He didn't mean to insult us."

The rest of the afternoon passed without incident,

although a minuscule amount of frigidity suggested the evidence of a cold war between the menfolk. Insults, deliberate or inadvertent, are tasteless things to swallow, especially when pride must be used as a seasoning. Nevertheless, there are occasions when such ingurgitating is essential to coexistence. One must compromise with oneself, as well as with one's fellows. Sometimes, I think it takes more courage to confess an error than maintain a right.

Three days were required for the completion of the fireplace and chimney, and I felt proud of my share in their construction. It had been hard work for hands accustomed to handling books, and they showed it. But books and bricks seem to go together like light and heat, a good novel and a cozy fire.

Monday morning the steam shovel groaned its way in by the north side of the barn. It screeched to a stop under the guidance of its young operator. He jumped enthusiastically from the cab and chatted for a few minutes with Wilmot. "I'm out of the service about a year. I bought this machine, and started in business for myself. I operated heavy equipment in the army." Without further conversation he began to measure.

"From the cellar foundation to the wall is a hundred twenty-four feet," he hollered to Wilmot. "We'll go down four feet for the trench." Wilmot waved his okay and the noisy work began. The ground was dotted with boulders, and the tough roots of old trees tested the tensile strength of steel cables. While both operator and machine labored, Wilmot set up a pipe-cutting and -threading machine in the coach house. He cut and threaded the first two sections of pipe. One piece had to reach from the water in the well to an elbow on another pipe coming in through a round opening. That connection was about two feet down from the top of the well. From there to the barn, it would be joined section to section.

Wilmot was in too much discomfort to get down in the well himself. He put the old ladder down and tied a rope around my waist, and said I could connect the pipes by following his instructions. I said, "I'm afraid to get into a well. I don't know how deep it is."

He replied, "You won't drown, the water is only about four feet. You could stand up in that. The water level is low at this time of the year." With much timidity, I survived the ordeal, and he tightened and cemented the joint. We then went back to the cutting and threading. Little metal curls piled around our feet. He would carry the length of pipe to the trench, and I would get down to cement and turn the pipe until it was tight. Then Wilmot would finish the tightening with the wrench. We worked furiously, connecting one length of pipe after another, watching it grow, until it was connected all the way from the well to the cellar foundation. The object was to have everything ready in the trench when the man got through excavating the hole for the septic system. The board of health required the well to be 150 feet from the septic tank, and in the opposite direction, so the well was north of the barn, and the septic tank was near the south corner, with the leaching field halfway down toward the brook. All those requirements were met. We wouldn't have any trouble there.

The sun was beating down on us. We were dripping wet from both perspiration and the ankle-deep water seeping into the trench from the underground springs. "We made it," said Wilmot as the steam shovel appeared around the corner and headed for the trench. It took him only a short time to push the loose soil back and fill in the trench. Wilmot paid the man, and they wished each other good luck.

I said, "Now we can go inside out of the sun, and get something to eat." Wilmot wiped his face with an old rag and agreed. A recently purchased two-burner electric plate made cooking more comfortable, away from the heat of the fire and sun. While we were eating, I said to Wilmot, "Don't ask me to do anything as dangerous as getting down in that well again. I was petrified. If that old ladder broke, I would still be down there. You wouldn't be able to get me out."

"That is why I tied the rope around you. If I couldn't pull

you out, I could go for help. There was nothing to worry about."

I tidied up things while Wilmot had a pipe. He also needed a painkiller. In about an hour, we resumed our work. It looked so easy now, just connect the water pipe to the pump in the cellar. The concrete foundation was not so easily broached. With sledgehammer and crowbar, he gradually broke through. He suggested that I go in the cellar and pull the pipe through the hole. I didn't have the strength to hold on to it.

He called me outside again. "Hold on to the pipe here. I'll go in and get it through." I sat on the bank of freshly dug, cool earth holding the pipe. Just then a bumblebee buzzed around my head. Startled, I jumped up, forgetting my duty, and the pipe slid out of the hole. Wilmot rushed out of the cellar. "Hold it like this," he roughly demonstrated. Then we heard a snap. He stood like a person in a trance, just looking at the ground. He almost whispered, "I think the break is right here." He picked up the shovel and dug until the damage was discovered. It was early evening before we finally connected pipe to pump, and watched the gauge on top of the tank register fifty pounds of pressure.

Having water on tap was one of our most important achievements. We were relieved of the drudgery endured carrying buckets and milk cans of water from the brook or well. A garden hose served as temporary plumbing and made it possible for me to improvise a dressing room in the far corner of the coach house. A large packing case covered with towels served as a dresser. While I was thus engaged, he observed my frequent trips to the fire for warm water.

"What are you doing?" he asked.

"Getting ready to take a sponge bath."

"A what?" Men too often take a woman's daintiness for granted, not realizing, perhaps, that daintiness is one part natural, and nine parts soap and water.

We ordered the bathroom fixtures and kitchen sink from the plumber in Collinsville. They were delivered the next day, and he, along with two helpers, went to work immediately. We now had the bathtub with shower, but just cold water. The hot water would come when we had a heating system installed with a hot water tank. The drawback was we couldn't put a heating system in a place with no windows installed upstairs, only subflooring down, and no insulation and no trim on the windows downstairs. All that work couldn't possibly be done before the cold weather set in.

Wilmot said, "We could buy a gas hot water heater, but there is no gas in the country." He said he would inquire about it. In the meantime, I had to heat the water. But at least it was on tap. That was a help.

I was halfway through my vacation and there was a tremendous amount of work remaining to be done before we could move in. The living room was beginning to take shape to assume a definite pattern of individuality. The four windows were in, the ceiling up, and the fireplace lacked only the tile hearth. That would be done after the hardwood floor was installed.

The next important job was to hang the front door. The large opening, which had at one time accommodated the sliding barn doors, on the overhead iron track, had to be shrunk to the size of a thirty-six inch household door. The overhead track was gone, so all Wilmot had to do was cut and nail the studs, cut and nail boards for the outside wall and put the clapboards on the new part. Then he started to install the door.

Putting in a door looked an easy job. There was the opening; here was the new mahogany door. First he had it upside down. It was a colonial entrance door, with a cross, so there was definitely an up and down to it. Then he had it inside out. But there were also the hinges. After considerable frustration, cursing and measuring, he got the hinges on the door lined up with those sections on the doorjamb, and he lifted it up for me to tap the top pin in place as he inserted the bottom one. Finally, the job was done and the door closed properly. Wilmot wiped his face, and sat on his nail barrel to have a smoke. He smiled, "That's a good piece of work, even if I do say so myself."

"How will you keep the door closed?" I asked. "There is no hardware on it, not even a doorknob."

"That will come later. The next time I go to Collinsville, I'll buy some nice fancy hardware, and a chime doorbell, too." Looking at him in amusement, I improvised some doggerel that seemed to suit the occasion.

> *The door is closed, the light is on,*
> *The fire is high, and cares are gone.*
> *I take a book, I settle down,*
> *And from my brow goes ev'ry frown,*
> *I turn a page, I turn two more.*
> *My eyelids fall. I slump, I snore.*

Sunday was made dreary by intermittent rain. Layers of thick fog huddled in the valleys, and it was hard to be cheerful and resolute, particularly when Wilmot was skirmishing against another assault by an illness that had lately grown more intense, more frequent, and of longer duration. Most of the day he lay in bed trying not to worry about his immobility, trying desperately not to be disheartened. Fortunately, he had asked Angelo, a young carpenter who lived near us in East Hartford, to come out and work for a few hours. "I'll keep to hell out of Angelo's way," he sadly remarked.

Angelo arrived at nine o'clock, and proved to be dependable and conscientious. I worked with him putting up the three-inch fiberglass insulation between the studding in the living room. It was uncomfortable material to handle. Tiny particles penetrated our clothing and caused persistent itching. It even got inside the canvas gloves. But we refused to be deterred by discomfort, and by late afternoon we had the eighteen-by-twenty-six living room adequately armored against the winter winds.

After Angelo finished for the day, I paid him, and he said he would be happy to come back another time if we needed him. Wilmot came out of the bedroom, and we talked as I cooked supper. The fireplace was going to ward off the dampness. I pulled over the old table and we ate in front of the fire. Wilmot took more medicine, filled his pipe and, as he sat there smoking, said, "If you get an old knife and pack some insulation all around the windows, that will make them good and tight. No draft can get in then. It will have to be done before the men come tomorrow to install the Sheetrock."

"I thought we were finished for the day," I said.

He sighed. "I don't want you to get too tired, but we do have a busy day coming up tomorrow." I knew by the look on his face that he was wishing he could do it himself. If it had to be done, it was just as well to get at it. I pulled some insulation apart and packed the space between the windows and walls. No wind could possibly pass that barrier.

In the morning the Sheetrock installers came and began work immediately. About an hour after that, the electricians arrived. They made slow progress. The chestnut beams were as hard as rock. Drills broke and men cursed. They were frustrated. They had to go back to the shop for more supplies. I couldn't understand why they had to drill through the beams; surely there was plenty of space in the rooms, and the wires would be in the walls, between the insulation and the Sheetrock. I realized that they had to bring up wires from the cellar, and put lights upstairs. The carrying beams were sixteen inches thick, as were the ones around the foundation. They had to go back to the shop and bring back their boss. His first greeting was "These post and beam construction buildings are lousy jobs." He drew some sketches and gave instructions. I was wondering if they would have to remove the temporary wiring they had installed for us. But I didn't interrupt them by asking questions.

When the men went to their lunch and had something to eat, I walked down to the brook alone, and Wilmot sat in the shade with his pipe. The woods smelled of wet earth and wild-flowers. The brook, drunken and imbibing, teetered over the rocks, and was in a mood for singing. The squirrels thought so too as they chattered and scrambled up and down the trees in their usual headlong manner. They had now become as tame as kittens, and equally as curious.

Wilmot didn't go back to bed while the men were working in the house. Many times I wished that the work had been let out on a contract. Teamwork, properly organized, conserves time and effort. Professionals doing the work would have eliminated many blunders. One snag that really bothered me was the kitchen sink. The window had been installed without making allowance for the sink. The result was incompatibility. They had to either raise the window or move the sink. It was easier to move the sink. Relocating the plumbing was a smaller job than cutting through the outside wall. So, the sink was moved to an inside wall. I learned that this sort of thing was a common occurrence, and could have possibly been avoided if the job had been blueprinted in advance. Such a log-ical, efficient procedure, however, is seldom adopted when people are doing the work themselves. We learned the hard way and, perhaps, were all the more elated when wrong was made right, and the day's schedule of accomplishment termi-nated without too much lost time, or temper.

THAT NIGHT, after I had Wilmot settled in bed and was all bathed and ready for a rest with the new Anya Seton book, I heard Mrs. Ferguson at the back door. She said I was wanted on the telephone, so we drove up to her house. The caller was my boss in the library. She said the part-time girl had left and asked if I could cut short my vacation. I small-voiced a yes.

I found Wilmot anxiously waiting. Why would anyone call me at night? He thought something had happened in the family.

"Everything is all right. But I have to go back to work tomorrow, the girl left."

"God damn the luck," he said, as we dressed and headed home.

Back in the library the next morning, the customers were unanimous in saying, "Oh, you look wonderful. How tanned you are. You must have had a grand time on your vacation. Did you take a trip? I never saw you look so rested." Under such a barrage of questions and affirmations, I was reduced to the familiar expedient of smiling assent without actually concurring with any one of them. I had learned early in life that the smiles which we practice and cultivate to smoothen our relations with fellow humans are part of the language of diplomacy. My regular customers knew I was out at the barn, and they were anxious to hear how much we had accomplished.

Wilmot stayed out in the country during the week, and I went with him Sunday and Monday. He picked me up after work on Saturdays. He said the place would soon be finished enough for us to move in.

8

$\mathcal{S}$unday, September 16: The long-awaited transition to country living had officially begun. Wilmot overburdened the car with boxes of dishes and innumerable small articles, and we got under way, some weeks sooner than originally planned. He said it was becoming difficult to act as chauffeur and hoped I would be able to join a car pool to get back and forth from work. There must be people up the hills of Barbertown working in Hartford, he said.

I spent the afternoon sweeping up plaster dust, wood shavings, and nails that had been hit with more vigor than accuracy, and storing away tools strewn helter-skelter by careless workmen. When everything was finally tidied away, and our new house looked reasonably presentable, I stood for a few minutes and looked around. The living room had walls, ceiling, trim on the windows, a beautiful, number-one selected oak floor and, best of all, a huge fireplace with bookcases floor to ceiling. Although the kitchen, bedrooms and bathroom had Sheetrock walls and ceilings, no stripping had been done. But these were not major obstacles to immediate occupancy.

Monday morning, back in East Hartford, we were up at five-thirty, ate a light breakfast and began loading the car with the remaining things that required delicate handling. We were not ready for the movers. At seven o'clock, they were in the driveway, those burly men to whom weight lifting is an art best performed with the obligate purple phraseology. In three hours, our worldly possessions were packed in the van. The expensive pieces were treated with considerable care, and we were hoping the unloading would be done with equal adroitness.

Wilmot thought it would be a good idea for me to reach the farm first. He would remain to clean up after the movers were finished. He had made arrangements with Lennie, a fellow in East Hartford, to go out and help him clear away some brush. He called and asked Lennie if I could ride out with him. In less than an hour I was working inside, making preparations for the movers, and Lennie was raking and cleaning up around the barn. He dismantled the outdoor fireplace and carried all the pieces up to the old foundation. While we were thus engaged, Wilmot drove in.

He looked around and exclaimed, "Where's the truck?" He walked out to the road and looked up and down. Forcing himself to be calm, he lit his pipe and sat on the back step. "It left long before I did. Where in hell is it?" He suggested that I drive up to the Fergusons' and phone the moving company. While I was dialing the company, Mrs. Ferguson made some tea and toast with her fresh raspberry jam made from the wild berries in the woods. It was a real treat.

She said, "We are neighbors now, why don't you call me Natalie, and my husband, Bob?"

I got right through to the dispatcher. He said, "Sorry, ma'am, the truck broke down out on Route 44. The men are repairing it. We will be there as soon as possible."

Wilmot wouldn't eat any lunch. He was disappointed and

exasperated. He impatiently walked up and down the driveway looking for a sign of the truck. It was early afternoon before he heard the frog-throated horn of the massive vehicle. Six hours had elapsed since the time we left town and the time everything was unloaded. Wilmot paid the men and offered each a can of beer. The driver said to his helpers, "It's okay, the smell will be worn off by the time we get back to the garage." They wished us good luck and drove away, hoisting their cans.

Men regard a woman's absorption with the minute details of interior decorating as a sort of harmless mania that occasionally disrupts the family budget, but nothing worse. However, they sometimes become irascible when an inflexible regimen of "Keep the house tidy" is imposed upon them. At this point, a knowledgeable wife discards some of her prohibitions and comforts herself with a couplet from a poem.

> While Romeos prefer to roam,
> Untidy husbands stay at home.

These reflections were marathoning through my mind as we assembled the beds and juggled furniture around in compliance with my varying choices of placement. We unrolled the two nine-by-twelve Oriental rugs lengthwise in the living room. The divan was placed against the wall facing the fireplace. The marble-top tables and lamps were set at each end of it. Two large wing chairs and tall plants completed that wall. The end of the room across the front had a large window looking out on the brook and rustic bridges. At one side of that window, we put the television, and at the other side, near the door going to the front hall, we placed the radio-stereo cabinet. Under the window, to break up the all-wood look, we put a velvet-covered low bench.

The back end of the room had the dining room set. The big hutch fit between the window and kitchen wall. The dining table and chairs were convenient to the kitchen. Between that corner and the fireplace was Wilmot's big chair and ottoman, and a table for his smoking supplies. The other side of the fireplace was a perfect spot for the big white leather chair and an embossed leather-top table, with a lamp completing that side of the room.

By now, it was after seven o'clock. We were hungry, but Wilmot said, "Let's get the kitchen stove up first." It was the big six-burner one, four front burners for gas, and two back ones for oil. He had a five-gallon container of oil that he bought the week before when he was in Collinsville. We would have to burn oil to cook with because he hadn't yet made arrangements for the bottled-gas people to deliver the propane. They told him a service man would have to come out to change the burners from regular gas to bottled. We were putting up the stovepipe when Natalie came in the back door. She was carrying a picnic basket. "Here," she said, "this is the best I could do in a short time. But, if you're hungry enough, it will taste good." She put a platter on the table. She removed the napkins, and there was a beautiful sight: broiled chicken and fresh vegetables, all ready to eat. We washed our hands and thoroughly enjoyed the dinner.

We reluctantly went back to work. Wilmot connected the pipe to the stove and, without too much fuss, fitted the pipe into the chimney flue. Then he filled the three-gallon jug and the stove was ready to light. "I didn't like that mason," said Wilmot, "but I will give him credit for doing a first-rate job. The fireplace draws beautifully, and I'm sure this flue and the one for the furnace will be just as good. That sure is a whopper of a chimney. How many bricks did it take?"

"Two thousand five hundred," I replied. "I know. I have the chapped hands to prove it."

When Natalie came back to collect her dishes, we talked about the possibility of me getting transportation back and forth to Hartford. Wilmot said, "I'll be worried about you driving back and forth to the city, especially on the icy roads and during snowstorms." He looked so tired and exhausted, I didn't reply. What I was thinking about commuting was better kept private.

Natalie said, "I know a woman who lives up in Ratlum Mountain. She has her own car and she takes riders. She works at G. Fox and Company, and the library is right near that. I'll call and ask her if she can accommodate another rider."

"Tell her I'll be going back to work Tuesday. These are the last few days of my vacation."

"I'll come down and let you know in the morning," Natalie replied as she left for home.

Wilmot looked pleased. "If you get a ride, I'll have the car. I can get most of the groceries at the Canton Center store, and also go to Collinsville for the materials I might need during the day."

I thought, He won't be using much materials from now on, but I said to him, "Let me help you get ready for bed and give you your medicine."

Tuesday morning, at twenty minutes to eight, I waited at the intersection of West and Barbertown roads. At a quarter to eight I heard a car coming down Barbertown. An old Ford pulled to the side of the road. A tall, pleasant woman leaned out the window. "Are you Mrs. MacNeill?"

I nodded and was invited to get in. Introductions followed. The driver was Inez, the passenger sitting next to her was Dierdre, a model at G. Fox, the nicest store in Hartford. She said to me, "I was sizing you up as we came down the road. I said to Inez, 'Who's the model around here, anyway?' How much do you weigh?"

"One hundred and ten pounds," I told her.

"How tall are you?" she inquired.

"Five feet six inches." I laughed, trying to hide embarrassment. Does a model visually weigh and measure every other woman? I wondered as I sat back and listened to Dierdre tell about her weekend at the Eastern States Exposition in West Springfield, Massachusetts. Her loquacity persisted until we reached the highway and the gas station, where our third passenger awaited us. She was introduced as Millie, another commuter. She was a lovely girl, imbued with all the warmth and personality that is traditionally Italian.

My first day as a commuter was fairly uneventful. Of course, my point of view as regards people and things had undergone subtle changes. I was beginning to think of myself as a country dweller. I felt, to put it bluntly, that I must serve the daily sentence of eight hours which is imposed upon us by the authority of economic necessity. But I was among the fortunate minority who liked doing what I did, liked meeting people, making new friends, and most of all, books.

The time passed pleasantly enough and, soon, as scheduled, I was homeward bound with my fellow riders. It was 6:45 P.M. when we got back to the starting point. Inez deposited me there, and I walked the three quarters of a mile up and down the grades of West Road. The thought ran through my mind that it was daylight now, but what would this be like on dark, stormy nights? At last, I was at the bridges, and home.

Wilmot was standing by the stove. He looked embarrassed as he pointed to the pot and said, "I was going to have your supper ready when you got home, but while I took a nap, it burned. You can cook bacon and eggs or something." I changed into slacks and a blouse and prepared supper. He seemed glad to have me home. The poor chap was in bed most of the day, weakened by pain.

At the table, we talked and ate in our usual amiable fashion, and I thought the occasion auspicious for a recurrent question. "Don't you think I had better give up the job and stay home with you, dear?"

I was answered with some acerbity. "Certainly not. You know you will have to rely on your job someday. We've been all through this before. Let's not say any more about it."

He was, of course, being logical, and properly concerned about my future. When supper was over, Wilmot returned to bed, and I washed the dishes and began unpacking some boxes. The good china was stacked on top of the hutch, and lesser items piled in a corner on the floor. He called to me. He needed a shot. Before long I went to bed thinking of the long walk up the road in the morning.

At lunchtime the next day, I remembered Wilmot's suggestion, "If you get some groceries, the nonperishable things, on your lunch hour, it won't be necessary for me to go to Collinsville."

I did some essential shopping and even found time for a quick lunch. Going home that night, car space was at a minimum. All four of us were bundle-laden. Dierdre had her omnipresent hatbox. Millie had bought a new suit. Inez had a bag with a pair of old shoes in it. In spite of the crowdedness, the ride home was pleasant and occasionally noisy with bursts of laughter from Dierdre, an irrepressible raconteur, who initiated what she called "the dirty half hour."

When I got out of the car, there was no sign of Wilmot. He said he would come up to meet me. I started walking, thinking he would be along any minute. The bags of groceries became heavier with each step. I had to put them down on the road several times to get a rest. There was never another car on the road, no one to give me a lift. This stop-and-go performance lasted until I reached the bridges. Leaving the bundles on the roadside, I went in the house to find Wilmot in bed. I returned to the road for the bundles. As I was putting things away, he awoke. "I'm sorry, honey, those new pills are so strong, I slept all day. Sit down and get a rest." He was so contrite, and looked weak and thin. He needed a good, hot meal. While supper was cooking, I lit the fire in the living room, and we ate in cozy comfort while watching television.

He asked, "How is the ride working? What did Dierdre have to say tonight?"

"She told us about a woman, a minister's wife, who was in the same room with her when she had her last baby. She said she asked the woman, 'Is this your first baby?' and the woman replied, 'No, this is my second. I got caught both times.'" That made him laugh.

The rest of the week, he was in bed and I was uneasy about him being in the house alone. One thing that worried me was that the medicine was potent. What if he should forget and take a second dose?

SUNDAY provided the opportunity to wash and dry heaps of assorted laundry. Wilmot's bed had to be changed two to three times a day. He had now become incontinent, a sad state of affairs for such a proud man. Little time was devoted to breakfast. I walked around outside, looking for some way to improvise a fireplace. A kettle and pots of water on the kitchen stove would not be adequate. The wash I had to do needed lots of hot water. Up near the old foundation there were a few whole bricks. I wheelbarrowed them down and made a fire ring. Another trip disclosed an old oil drum. It was clean, dry, and free of wasps' nests. It fit safely on the bricks. I filled it from the hose that Wilmot kept connected to an outside tap at all times. "Just in case of fire," he said.

He was procrastinating about insurance. He realized the need for protection on the buildings, but just the mention of an insurance man got him upset. He would never let an agent in the house. He told Tom not to have a collector come about his policy, to mail it to the company every six months or once a year. Keep collectors away from the house, he said, it was embarrassing to have someone come to your door asking for money. The mention of life insurance got him more riled than talk of property protection. "You put your money in the bank for a rainy day," he said, "and don't pay for their elaborate buildings and fancy offices." Consequently the only life insurance he owned was a paid-up $2,000 policy. He bought that many years ago as a favor to a friend who was getting started in the business.

Before long, I was carrying in buckets of hot water, and the washing machine was working all afternoon. The hot sun and the lovely breeze dried the things quickly.

MONDAY was a repetition of Sunday, more bedclothes to be washed and dried. I said to Wilmot, "The work would be so much easier if we had hot water in the house. Could you buy an electric hot water heater?"

"I'll think about it," he said as he went outside. When I looked out to see what he was doing, he was over in the woods pruning an old apple tree. When I went out to bring in the clothes, he called to me. "Come over here and see the beautiful wildflowers." There was a patch of red blooms hidden by the tall weeds. It was hot standing there in the woods and the mosquitoes were devouring me.

"Why don't you come over and sit on the step, in the shade? I'll bring you out a glass of milk."

"Wouldn't that be a lovely spot for a vegetable garden when it is cleared?" he said. It was heartbreaking to hear him talking of a garden when we both knew he wouldn't be here in the spring.

$\mathcal{M}$rs. MacNeill, we are going to move into an apartment and we are just heartbroken to have to give up our beautiful dog." Tears welled up in the customer's eyes as she continued, "She is a German shepherd, beautifully trained. We have had her for five years. You just moved to the country; could you give her a home? If you took her, we would know she was well cared for and loved."

I experienced one of those impulses that cannot be denied. Before I knew it, I said, "Don't worry about her, Mrs. Hoyt, I'll be glad to have her. We have been talking about getting a dog. She will have lots of room to play, and my husband will be with her all day."

"Her name is Smoky," smiled Mrs. Hoyt, as she went away in a more cheerful frame of mind.

The following Sunday I was officially adopted by Smoky. It was obviously a case of love at first sight when Mrs. Hoyt's two sons brought out their pet. We all went in the living room and sat down. The boys felt as badly as their mother did about parting with Smoky. They told us about the cute little things she did. They bragged about her like a father talking about his children. The emotional strain seemed to lessen when they saw Smoky walk around Wilmot, looking up at him as if she knew he was ill and needed her love and protection. Then she came over to me and put her head in my lap and wagged her tail. The boys smiled at each other and thanked us for taking her. From that moment on, she definitely resigned from dog-dom and became one of the family.

After working hours she was always with me, indoors or out. She seemed to know when it was time for me to come home. Wilmot said she kept going to the back door and listening. In her own way she seemed to understand that he could not go outside and romp with her. When he sat by the fire smoking his pipe, she was at his feet. When he went to bed, she stayed by the bedside. If he dropped his glasses, book or newspaper, she picked them up in her mouth. She was company for him, and I was happy to have her.

Our car pool had now acquired a fifth member, a hand-some, sweet-dispositioned woman who, in a short time, became one of my best friends. Medine Randall was employed in the pharmacy at G. Fox and Company. We all enjoyed having her with us. She was generous with her good advice and good cheer whenever there was need for one or both. It was she who organized our "paint-bucket picnic." She did it with only a few words.

"What would you girls think of it, if we held a painting spree on Sunday? I don't think the good Lord would frown if we did a good turn for our new neighbor." Everyone agreed.

"Sure, that would be fun. What are we going to paint?"

"Not the whole house," said Medine in her soft voice. "Just the living room in Mary's barn. I thought it would be nice to have it all prettied up for Thanksgiving."

There was unanimous agreement and the girls promised to bring their husbands and paintbrushes. When I told Wilmot of the proposed contribution to our labors, he was delighted and said, "I knew people in the country were friendly, but who would expect anything like this? They are giving up their Sunday when I'm sure they must have many things to do."

Sunday afternoon, our brigade of painters arrived. Medine was dressed in a pair of slacks and a gray blouse. Millie and Inez wore blue jeans and men's work shirts, and Dierdre was dressed in dramatic black, with a large silk scarf pinned in a bow on her shoulder. The men were dressed casually and seemed eager to get the job started. In a surprisingly short time our concerted efforts began to show results.

Inez and I worked on one wall until her husband said, "If Mrs. Mac will help me, we can put up the Sheetrock in the front bedroom." I turned over my paintbrush to Inez and went in the bedroom to help her husband. We managed to get the ceiling nailed up, but there was no time left to do the taping of the seams.

Meanwhile, Dierdre's husband, who was an electrician, went up in the attic to install the TV antenna. He said, "It would spoil the appearance of a colonial house to have a TV mast on the roof."

By five o'clock, Operation Paintbrush was successfully accomplished. Everyone was pleased with the transformation. The living room wall was now a soft bayberry gray, which contrasted beautifully with the rugs and furniture, and would be even nicer when I had time to remake the cranberry bark-cloth drapes. The room had an inviting, comfortable look.

Our volunteer interior decorators had brought with them two dozen doughnuts, a pound of coffee and a bushel of apples purchased from the orchard up the road. Inez made the coffee, and Millie and I set the dining table. It was simple fare that lay before us, but plain food eaten in an atmosphere of comradeship and merry conversation gains in digestibility whatever it may lose in appearance. We coaxed Wilmot to come out of the bedroom, and he sat by the fire with an afghan wrapped around his legs. As we sat there, relaxing and chatting, it occurred to me, and perhaps to the others as well, that there is no satisfactory substitute for conversation among friends.

Our painting party finally reached adjournment. Dishes were washed, furniture dusted, rugs vacuumed, and painting tools washed and wrapped to be taken home. Wilmot could hardly find words to thank the men and women who had given up their Sunday to help us.

I helped him get back to bed and gave him his medicine. He would be comfortable for a few hours. In the past few weeks his pain was more intense. He needed morphine at about ten o'clock at night, and at about two and six in the morning.

10

By the end of November, Wilmot's condition had grown steadily worse. He spent most of the day in bed. I would change the bed and get him as comfortable as possible before I left for work. He couldn't eat much, and what he did eat didn't stay down. All he wanted during the day was a thermos of coffee and something light. He had the pills, magazines, radio and pipe on the table next to the bed. He did get up to smoke, which relieved my mind a little. And he had the coffee in the thermos, so he didn't go near the stove.

One morning as I was leaving, he said, "I want you to call the doctor today. Tell him I can't keep that goddamn morphine down. Ask him if he can prescribe something else. I can't lie around all day. I have things to do. Tell him I have a feeling that my time is running out." He put his arm around me. "Come on now, don't carry on, you have a ride to catch."

As I walked up the road, I tried to pull myself together. I stopped a minute and watched a pheasant and her brood of little ones cross the road. I hoped that she would get under some bushes before a hunter saw her. The leaves rustled and the air was cool and crisp with the smell of frost.

The car stopped and Inez said, "Gee, you look terrible. Are you sick?"

"Not sick," I said, "just terribly upset."

"I wouldn't be able to take care of a sick man; why don't you put him in a hospital?"

"I'll take care of him as long as I can, or as long as he will let me. It's been eight years since he had the first operation," I replied.

"What did the doctor say about him being out in the country trying to get a house built when he is in so much pain?" Millie asked.

"The doctor agreed that it would be better for Wilmot to have something to do, something to think about, instead of the pain."

When we picked up Medine, she said the same thing. "You look terrible. Why didn't you stay home today?"

I took an early lunch hour in order to catch the doctor before he left his office. The nurse told him that I was on my lunch hour and he came to the phone right away. I told him in a shaky, emotional voice what Wilmot wanted to know. "Well, to tell you the truth, Mrs. Mac, he won't be in the land of the living much longer. How is he doing on the morphine?"

"He wants to know if you can prescribe something else, Doctor. He can't keep the morphine, or anything else, down. Should I try to get him in to see you?"

"There is no need for him to come in town. The only thing we can do for him from now on is keep him comfortable. I will call in a prescription for Demerol. He might be able to keep that down."

"I would like to stay home with him, but he won't hear of it," I told the doctor. "He says I have to hold on to my job."

"I'll take a run out one of these days and have a talk with him." I thanked the doctor and went over to Sage-Allens' to get some lunch, but couldn't eat it.

When I went back to the library, my helper asked, "What did the doctor say?" When I told her, she said, "The poor guy will be better off."

We didn't talk anymore.

There were more customers than usual. It seemed everyone was in town Christmas shopping. When the rush was over, she said, "Go get yourself a cup of tea, and take your time."

The afternoon dragged on. I was beginning to lose patience with people. One woman asked for a copy of *My Brother, My Enema*. Without bothering to tell her the correct title, I gave her *My Brother, My Enemy*. Another asked for something romantic. "I never married," she said. "I traveled the ocean thirteen times. Haven't you got what you in the United States call sex appeal?" I gave her a Faith Baldwin, a light romance.

When I got out of the car at Barbertown Road that night and started the long, dark walk home, I was wondering what it would be like later on, in the storms. There was never a person or car in sight, though I was never nervous. I knew the noises in the bushes were made by little animals. Sometimes, I could see little eyes flashing in the dark.

When I opened the kitchen door, Wilmot was standing by the kitchen stove. He had his pants on under his bathrobe. "It is quarter after seven. What kept you? I was getting dressed to go up the road looking for you. I thought you must have fallen or gotten hurt in the dark."

"I am tired. It took me longer than usual. How are you feeling?"

"Groggy from all the dope I'm taking. Sit down and I'll try and get you some supper."

Instead, I got him to sit down while I changed clothes and cooked supper. We didn't eat much. I was dreading the inevitable questioning about the doctor. I watched Wilmot light his pipe and sit by the fire. Here it comes, I thought, what will I say?

"Come over here," he said, as he patted the ottoman. I sat

beside him. "Do you remember me asking you to call the doctor?"

"Yes."

"Why don't you tell me what he said?"

"He said he will come out and see you some day soon."

He picked up my hand and held it between his. He was conscious of my distress. "Listen dear, I know I don't have much time left. You have to tell me what the doctor said. I have to know."

I sobbed, "Three months. But we will make every minute count."

11

*T*he first heavy snow of the winter was falling. I looked out the front window at a moonlit world. Every bush was robed in ermine for the occasion. Beautiful to look at, I thought, but it will be a hard, slippery walk up the road in the morning. At least I wouldn't have to walk it alone. Natalie was working at G. Fox for the Christmas season.

She tapped on the back door at eight in the morning. She was dressed for the cold. She was wearing sealskin boots, a knitted cap and a long woolen scarf, wrapped twice around her neck. "You had better dress in warm clothes, it is zero out."

"It's near zero in too," I told her. As we walked up the road, there was not a footprint or tire mark to dirty the freshly plowed surface. The air was so sweet, you could almost taste it. But our noses were pinched with the frost. I had heavy clothes and lined boots on, but the cold was penetrating. We were happy to see our chauffeur coming.

That night as we were eating supper, I heard a car drive in. It was Tom. He had his car garaged in East Hartford while he was away. He said, "It started up as soon as I turned the key. Didn't even need a battery charge. Good thing it was indoors." It was a delight to see him. We sat around the fire until midnight. He was excited and full of news about the trip. He had taken hundreds of slides, and was anxious to get them processed and show them to us. He brought us presents from Egypt and Africa. It was fascinating to hear firsthand about the people in Spain, Italy, Greece and the Holy Land.

Tom stayed home all week. He sawed wood for the fireplace and helped all he could, but everything outside was under snow. He couldn't do anything but shovel a path to the front door. The second week, he made several trips into Hartford to see friends and go to the movies. Then he grew disenchanted with country living and said, "This is for the birds. I'm going to San Diego."

"San Diego is the place for young people," I replied, "and this cold house is not good for you. You have such trouble with headaches."

"Can you manage from now on? I know things are getting worse. I can see that for myself. Will you be okay?"

I assured him, "I'll be okay. We are keeping in touch with the doctor." He again packed his things and left for California.

Our new friend in Collinsville, Medine Randall, said she would have her husband, Tony, come up to the house whenever he got home early. He was athletic coach at the Wethersfield prison. This time of the year the men were not outside much and Tony had fewer games to coach. Wilmot was happy to have another man to talk to during the day. It was also a relief for me, knowing that at least part of the day there was someone with him. Unfortunately, by the first part of December, Wilmot's condition became critical. He could not retain food. Even a drink of water would not stay down. The bedclothes had to be changed several times a day.

"You can't go on like this. I'm too much of a burden to you. Think of yourself for once. You need your sleep, you can't be up with me all night and go to work the next day.

Another thing, consider how embarrassing it is for me to have my wife cleaning up after me. I want you to call Dr. Wahro and ask him to make arrangements for me to go to the veterans hospital. I've paid out so much money to the Hartford hospital over the years, this time I'm going to Veterans."

I interrupted. "I don't want anyone else taking care of you. I want to do it myself. If I were sick, wouldn't you take care of me?"

"Will you please stop talking like that and do what I ask?"

The next Saturday while I was packing his bag and carefully tucking his army discharge and other papers in the side pocket of his jacket, the ambulance came.

Two white-coated orderlies rapped on the back door. Smoky rushed at them when I called, "Come in." I had to hold her by the collar as the men went in the bedroom. When they came through the kitchen with Wilmot on the stretcher, I had to get down on my knees and put my arms around her.

"Never mind me," Wilmot said, "hold on to Smoky." Then I heard him say to the men, "Just a minute, fellows. I want to take a look at the brook. I'll never see it again."

Natalie heard the ambulance pulling away and she came running down the road. I was sitting on the kitchen floor with my arms around Smoky—me crying and the dog howling. Natalie made a pot of tea, and we sipped and talked. "You shouldn't be alone tonight. Why don't you call your brother?"

I took the suggestion and called brother Bill in Medford, Massachusetts. He said as soon as his wife, Mary, came back from shopping, she would pack a few things and they would be here for the weekend. Natalie said, "I'm glad they are coming. I'll be back later."

I put on boots and heavy clothes, and took Smoky for a walk along the brook. She jumped about and bit at the snow. Wilmot had been gone only two hours. He had been in and out of hospitals many times before, but this time it was different. I knew he would not come home and so did he. I felt more alone than I had ever been.

A vital part of my life was now missing. My little world had grown smaller. There is inescapable sadness in the realization that all our possessions, human and material, are really not possessions at all. They are merely things borrowed, and subject to immediate recall at a moment's notice. But there is little to be gained by feeling sorry for oneself, or others. A more practical approach to such emergencies is to help oneself, or others, by rearranging what is left of one's life in closer conformity with realities, by submerging one's sense of loss in a veritable sea of activity. We may often be defeated, but we should never get downhearted.

> *It matters not how straight the gate,*
> *How charged with punishment the scroll,*
> *I am the master of my fate,*
> *I am the captain of my soul.*
>   W. E. HENLEY

In the midst of all this philosophizing, Natalie appeared on the scene. While I was washing bedclothes, she polished silver and set the table with the best linen cloth and silver candlesticks.

"There now, doesn't that look nice? I'll send one of the boys down to carry some logs over near the door."

While I was making beds and preparing for weekend guests, she refilled the oil burner jug for the kitchen stove. At least a part of the house would be warm. Dinner was ready at seven o'clock, but not a sign of anyone. A little after eight Smoky began barking. I stepped outside and looked. A fox dashed out of the coach house and headed for the woods. Waiting is such an ordeal, and trying to keep a cooked dinner from spoiling is an aggravation. At nine o'clock a car pulled in the driveway with its cargo of family. What a relief.

Ordinarily, brother Bill has a most scintillating personality, but on this occasion his buoyant words of cheerfulness appeared to have been rehearsed for my benefit. He was making a determined effort to give my spirits a boost, to add a little muscle to my morale. He put his arms around me and said, "We were lost for hours on these country roads. All we saw were foxes and rabbits. This must be great hunting country."

Meanwhile, sister-in-law Mary and Billie Junior were busy bringing in things from the car. Billie said, "Aunt Mary, do you have any worms? I would like to go fishing in the morning if the brook is not frozen over."

"We might be able to dig under the snow and find some in a pile of rotted leaves," I told him. Like all ten-year-old boys, the thought of fishing through the ice intrigued him.

Brother Bill asked Mary, "How do you like the place?"

"Well, personally, I wouldn't live here if they gave me the place for nothing."

Bill laughed. "Don't worry, old girl, they won't."

Billie Junior was more enthusiastic. "Gee, I never saw such a big living room. Can I put some logs on the fire?"

I served the roast and vegetables. Being kept warm for hours had robbed them of flavor and appeal. Bill made the tea and brought in fresh biscuits from the oven. The family seemed to enjoy the meal, but I couldn't eat much. My throat was aching from trying to hold back tears. After dinner, father and son watched television. Mary and I did the washing up. It was nearly midnight before anyone thought of bed.

Mary had some misgivings about sleeping in an unfinished room. She asked, "How can I get undressed when there are no window shades to pull down? Someone might look in."

"There are no prowlers around here," I told her, "only animals in search of food, or perhaps an owl, who doesn't give a hoot about anybody." To put her mind at rest, I thumbtacked an old pair of drapes over the windows, remarking as I did so, "Mary, I thought I was lucky to have windows in here, never mind the shades. Upstairs there is only cardboard tacked to the window openings."

She and Billie Junior got in my bed, and Bill got in

Wilmot's. I made a place for myself on the living room divan. Just as I settled down, Bill popped his head in. "Mary is afraid of the electric blanket. You had better go in with her, and I'll sleep here." We exchanged quarters, and I joined Mary.

"What did you do to keep warm before you bought these things? Aren't you afraid of them?"

"I was the first night, but it was so comfortable I soon overcame my fear. You would too, if you had to dress for bed the way I did."

She thought the idea of dressing for bed was some sort of joke, until I gave her a résumé of that remarkable routine. "I used to put a flannelette blanket over and under the cold sheets, put on a pair of men's flannelette pajamas, wrap my feet in a pair of men's long drawers, tie a heavy scarf around my head, and put on a pair of gloves."

Her look of incredulity was something to see. "Why gloves?" she asked.

"My hands were so cold, I had to wear gloves if I wanted to read in bed." That did it. I can still hear her laughing. And I wasn't trying to be funny.

"What about Wilmot?" she asked. "Did he feel cold?" She was surprised to hear that he didn't always turn on his blanket. He had a fever most of the time, and was too warm.

"Did he get up at night to take medicine?" she asked.

"No. He called me when he was in pain, and I gave him the morphine, and later on he had a prescription for Demerol. He usually had medicine before he went to bed, and around two in the morning, and again around six in the morning. He took the pills himself when I was at work."

"You didn't get any sleep yourself, did you?" she asked.

Mary got up at five in the morning and aroused Bill. "Get up, we have to go look for a church. I want to go early and get it over with."

I reminded her that the church was only a few miles away in Collinsville, and there wouldn't be any service until seven o'clock. Nevertheless, they cooked breakfast and got ready. Billie Junior wanted to stay home and play in the woods, but his mother took him along.

After church they had some hot coffee, and I called the hospital to inquire about visiting hours. A doctor answered the telephone. He said, "We will be working with your husband all day. He is in serious condition, and we have to ascertain what will be the best course of treatment. It will be more beneficial to him and to us if you do not visit him today. Give us a call this evening. We may be able to tell you something then." We were disappointed, but we certainly did not want to go over and be in the way.

"How far away from here is the hospital?" Bill asked.

"The ambulance driver told me it is about thirty-eight miles," I replied.

"As long as we can't go to the hospital, let's put up the Sheetrock in the back bedroom. The studs are already there. We can do a lot before dinner."

We started the bedroom job while Mary defrosted the refrigerator, washed off the stove and busied herself getting lunch. Billie Junior went outside to play with Smoky. He tried fishing with pieces of bread for bait, but didn't catch a trout. He then took an ax and broke up several oak barrels. They made a wonderful fire. He asked me who cut up all the logs in the coach house.

"A man came with a chain saw and cut up all the broken tree limbs and dead trees. I have a cord of dry logs."

"How much is a cord?" he asked.

"A cord is a pile four feet wide, four feet high, and eight feet across. That is what the man told me."

Bill, noticing how industrious his wife was, commented, "The little old Dutch Cleanser Kid, herself."

Night came too soon. It was time for them to return home. Bill's parting words were "I think you'll have a lovely place here before long. Don't you agree, Mary?"

She looked at him and repeated her previous statement. "I

told you, dear, I wouldn't live here if they gave me the place for nothing." Then, turning to me, she asked, "What would you do if you took a heart attack in the middle of the night?"

"I don't have time for heart attacks, Mary."

"Well, what would you do if someone tried to break in?"

"No one would get in here with Smoky around."

"They would shoot her first."

Bill took her by the arm. "Come on, old girl, let's get going. It's a long drive home. And I will say this much for you, you like to leave people in a good frame of mind."

12

*L*oneliness that is chosen voluntarily is not really loneliness at all, because it is something sought after, something desirable for a variety of reasons, good, not so good, and good for nothing. The hermit in his cave is a refugee from humanity who seeks to establish a beachhead on the shores of eternity, believing that those who follow the path of renunciation achieve a closer affinity with things spiritual, that a man cannot love too much things material and still see himself as a suitable candidate for a corner lot in the suburbs of heaven.

In my particular situation, loneliness was thrust upon me. I was a victim of circumstances, and circumstances do not change, at least, not retroactively. My first night alone in my partially completed home remains unforgettable. An odd thing about human nature is our tendency to recall unpleasant incidents much more vividly than those which gave us pleasure. We do so, I think, for the simple reason that pain writes with a heavier hand upon the scrolls of memory. Happiness has a lighter, more evanescent touch.

I was alone. Worse than that, I was lonely. I sat by the fire, walked from room to room, sat down again, and picked up some magazines and tried to occupy my mind with the latest ideas in decorating. Someday, the rest of the walls would have to be painted. Blue-spruce green would be nice for the big sunny bedroom, rose for the front hall, pale yellow for the smaller bedroom. In the bathroom, the stunning redbird would complement the white ceramic tile with black trim that was already installed in the tub enclosure. The rough plumbing had been installed upstairs for future expansion. For at least a little while, I managed to lose myself in a Technicolored mirage. Eventually, it was time to go to bed. Everything was so quiet. The sounds made by the little animals were now perfectly audible. I could hear them chewing on the winter squash and other vegetables in the cellar. Wilmot had gathered all the vegetables that would keep and moved them in burlap bags from his garden in East Hartford. There were also little things running around upstairs. Quiet and noise seem to be interdependent in the somewhat paradoxical sense that the presence of one is made noticeable by the diminution of the other. That is to say, it is difficult to hear quiet unless one hears noise at the same time, not a lot of noise, but enough to know that silence is predominant.

Smoky was sound asleep on her blanket in the kitchen and was surprised when I invited her to join me. Having her close to my bed would make me feel more at ease, I thought. But it didn't work that way. Immediately after I turned off the light, she jumped up on the empty twin bed and began to howl. I knew why she did it. Dogs miss their loved ones as keenly as humans do. In the canine world, a certain kind of low, plaintive whining denotes a state of mind commonly described as melancholic. Smoky was undoubtedly disturbed by the absence of her master. Fortunately, her lamentations gradually subsided, and toward dawn both of us finally fell asleep.

Morning, when it came, was never more welcome. There is nothing quite so reassuring as the light of day, particularly when the sun is shining uninhibited by clouds and fog. Day had come, and with it, resurgence of hope, of renewed determination to endure, survive and surmount the vicissitudes of life. That seems to be the only philosophy of living which helps keep one's dignity and self-respect intact and durable. Such, at least, has been my own experience. Perhaps that is why I like to recite my favorite prayer at morning, on such occasions. It is a simple expression of faith that has been an unfailing source of comfort through the years.

> *A quiet life, and happy, Glory be,*
> *When morning comes I wake to see*
> *The sun explore a windowpane*
> *So speckled by the summer rain*
> *That I can garner with my eyes*
> *Diamonds quarried from the skies;*
> *Glittering jewels that poets prize.*
> *A quiet life, and happy. Give to me*
> *No other boon, and I will be*
> *Content to seek no further gain*
> *Than harmony of heart and brain;*
> *Oh I will be content to prize*
> *Simple things, and rare, and wise*
> *This prayer, I make unto the Lord,*
> *That what I ask, be my reward.*

WE NOW had a new driver as a temporary substitute for Inez, who was in Maine for a vacation. She was a little woman about five feet tall, and she drove a brand-new car. She was a courteous driver and collected her riders closer to their houses. She picked Natalie and me up in front of my driveway, and thus spared us the long, cold walk. The first morning she was slightly behind schedule, and being somewhat flustered by haste, she had to spend time adjusting the cushions beneath and behind her. While doing so, she said, "I'm sorry I'm late. I had to get one of the neighbor's pigs out of the bedroom before I left."

"How did the pig get in the house?" I asked.

"The kids went out and left the back door open, and one of Bud Rainey's pigs got in." The name Bud Rainey was familiar to all of us who had the radio on at five-thirty in the morning. He often talked about his farm and about country living, but he never mentioned the name of the town. I was surprised to hear that he was only a few miles up the road in North Canton.

She seemed to be a happy-go-lucky person, and the ride in town was pleasant in a warm, new car. When we got out at the parking lot, she said, "I smell snow in the air. I hope it won't be stormy when we get out tonight."

It was busy in town. The stores were now open six days a week for the Christmas rush. Carols were played continuously from morning until the stores closed, and the Salvation Army people stood shivering in the cold, guarding their cauldrons of compassion.

Big, feathery flakes of snow were falling as we started home. It didn't appear to be the coming of a storm. It was like a Christmas snowfall. Driving wasn't too bad in the city, but when we came to the foot of Avon Mountain, the cars couldn't make the grade and were slipping and sliding all over the road. Our driver had new snow tires which enabled her to climb the mountain, but going down the other side, the car went from one side of the road to the other. The snowplows and sanding trucks were not even out yet. They were required to wait until the snowfall reached four inches before they started to work. This snow was wet, and freezing on the roads, making driving treacherous. It took four hours to reach Canton Center. She let us out at Barbertown Road.

She said, "I'm sorry, but I'm afraid to go down West Road. I might skid over the bridges into the brook."

We were thankful to have gotten home at all. If I didn't get home, what would Smoky do? With no one to let her out or feed her, and no one home to refill the oil jug, there would be no heat at all in the house, and the pipes would freeze. And, if we couldn't get home, Medine wouldn't be able to get up from Collinsville.

All these things were going through my head as we slipped, slid and fell on the unplowed road. Natalie said, "Thank God, we made it. If we didn't get home tonight, though, the boys would have gone down to take care of Smoky."

I said, "I forgot about the kids, but I was worrying about the oil for the stove, besides thinking about Smoky. I'm beginning to wonder about country living."

Natalie laughed. "I'm glad we didn't have groceries to carry tonight. They would be all over the road."

I found Smoky's water frozen in her dish on the kitchen floor. The stove had been out for hours. She frolicked in the snow while I brought in the oil and logs for the fireplace, and refilled the oil jug.

Overnight the storm turned into a blizzard, and by morning both front and back doors were knob-deep in snow. With the exception of the kitchen and living room, the rest of the house was unbearably cold. The explanation was simple: The plywood cover over the stairwell wasn't heavy enough to keep the wind from blowing down into the front hall. Every hour or so, I buffeted my way through the snowdrifts as far as the coach house to get more logs and struggle back indoors.

The snow fell all day. The roads became impassable and only the hardiest souls, the farmers who had to milk and feed their stock, ventured outside. Just before dark, the weight of the snow on the cellar bulkhead door snapped the hinges and it fell into the basement. I now had Arctic wind blowing up from below, as well as coming down the stairwell. The cellar door would have to be replaced as soon as possible. Snow was drifting down the hatchway. I phoned our neighbor, Bob Ferguson, and described the situation. He came down a short time later and, after considerable effort, was able to put the door back in place. The hinges, however, were twisted out of shape and worthless. It was the best he could do under the circumstances.

After chatting a few minutes about the severe winters up here in the hills, he said, "Just wait until you see the beauty of the spring, with all the old apple trees in bloom. Give us a call if you run into any more trouble."

> *While bone-dry leaves from summer's book*
> *Were dancing weirdly down the lane,*
> *A brawling winter came and shook*
> *His fist against my window pane.*
>
> *Unworried by his warlike air,*
> *I gestured back at him, and said,*
> *"Just wait, you bleak, Old Buccaneer,*
> *And spring will spike your frosty head."*

By evening, the snow had stopped falling and the wind died down. The stars flickered through latticed clouds. My latest contest with the elements had come to an end, but not my worries, nor my apprehensions. A disturbing thought teased my mind. What would I do if I got a call from the hospital—how would I ever get there? To lessen my anxiety, I telephoned and the nurse said, "He has had a lot of medication to keep him comfortable, and he doesn't know if you are here or not. If he asks for you, I will tell him there has been a bad storm and you are snowed in. Don't worry, we are doing all we can for him." Her words had a calming effect.

Wearied by the hard work of shoveling snow and carrying wood, I relaxed for a few minutes by the fire and was surprised to note that I had so many muscles that could ache simultaneously. In spite of all the hard work, I had no appetite and found myself unable to listen to the radio or read. I was obviously being plagued by both nervous and physical fatigue, and in such cases, sleep is the most effective remedy. As I began readying for bed, a visit to the bathroom to get some hand lotion provided another shock for my already ragged nerves. On the wall, directly above the basin, I saw a spider, not an ordinary spider, but a big black, furry monstrosity. For a few seconds I was powerless to move. I stood looking at it fascinated, and at the same time horrified. Then I remembered the spray gun that was lying on the floor in the front hall. It took a lot of spraying to destroy the repulsive visitor. The thought that there might be more of its brethren lurking in hidden places was frightening, and so I sprayed the walls, closet, floor and ceiling, as well as the hallway. When that was done I got out the encyclopedia in an effort to determine whether or not spiders of that size and appearance were poisonous. My research was fruitless.

Someone once told me that hot milk helps induce sleep. I was in an experimental mood, ready to try anything for relaxation, so I heated some milk and poured it into a warm cup. Then I went in to bed, propped myself up on the pillows, drank the recommended soporific, snuggled under the warm blanket and tried to read. In a short time I was warm and comfortable. The book dropped from my hands as I dozed. Smoky dutifully picked it up and placed it on the bed.

It seemed like only a few seconds since I had turned the light off and gone to sleep, when I was awakened by a vibrating noise. I could hear the pump in the cellar groaning. Running out to the kitchen I turned the taps on, and they gustily exhaled air, nothing else. I had to do something fast, but what? Getting down in the cellar was the first thing to do. I put on warm clothes and boots, went outside and tried to remove the recently replaced door. I found to my dismay that it had become frost welded, and I couldn't budge it. Meanwhile, the pump continued its groaning. Hurrying back into the house I put some papers and logs in the fireplace, and while warming my numbed fingers, wondered how I was going to escape this latest predicament. I thought of the telephone. The operator was most cooperative.

"Don't you know how to shut off the pump?" she asked.

"I do, but the cellar hatchway door is frozen. I can't get it open," I replied.

"In that case, I'll try and get a state trooper to you. That is, if I can locate one at two o'clock in the morning."

Minutes later the operator called back. "I've located a trooper. Give me directions how to get there. He will start out right away." I had never heard more welcome words.

Not long afterward, my one-man rescue squad arrived. He had no trouble finding the place. I had all the lights on. He parked his jeep on the road and scrambled on foot to the back door. I had to hold Smoky by the collar while letting the officer in.

His first questions were "What's the matter? Why are you up here in the woods alone?" When I explained that my husband was in Rocky Hills Veterans Hospital critically ill, his interrogative manner changed swiftly.

"I'm sorry," he said. "Now show me where the cellar door is, and I'll try to get down to pull the plug before the pump burns out."

He was a big man, tremendously strong. The door was a tough opponent, but not tough enough to defy the strong arm of the law. He finally got down in the cellar. It was such a relief to have the vibrating stop and the threat of fire removed. The trooper asked for a box of salt. I gave it to him wondering what he had in mind. To my surprise, he poured the contents down the kitchen sink drain.

"Your pipes are frozen, that is why the pump kept running. It couldn't draw any water from the well."

"I wish I had some water to make you a cup of tea, officer."

He replied, "I'll get some snow and melt it. That's what we did when I was in Alaska."

We had tea and cookies and he said, "I have to call in and report." His mission of mercy completed, the kind and courteous state trooper left. He acknowledged my gratitude. "Oh, it's all in day's work, or should I say, a night's work. We spend as much time helping people as we do arresting them."

I brought in some more snow and melted it, to wash up and get ready for work, if we could drive in town. The snow-plows were working all night, but the drifts were high. The driving would be treacherous. At seven o'clock I started calling plumbers, but no luck. It seemed nearly everyone in town had the same trouble. As one fellow said, "The whole town is frozen up."

The state trooper came back while I was telephoning. I told him, "I can't get a plumber. Most of the people in town have the same trouble."

"If your dog will let me stay awhile, I'll see what I can do." He smiled.

"She knows you now," I said. I left the library number in case he, or anyone else, had to get in touch with me.

Our driver was on time as usual. She said it took a long time to dig the car out. Her nephew was with her, in case we had any trouble on the road.

Natalie came along at the same time. "How did you make out last night?" she inquired. I told her about the pipes freezing and the state trooper coming to help, and that he was in the house now. We were introduced to the nephew, and his aunt suggested that he, Larry, could come down tonight and help.

"Won't soak you much," he said, and so I agreed.

Our driver's skilled hands maneuvered the car down the slippery hills and sleek roads, and there was frequent changing into second gear to avoid sliding into snowbanks.

While awaiting the arrival of the would-be plumber that night, a latter-day Diogenes equipped with a blowtorch, eager to defrost for cold cash, I started preparing something to eat, again melting snow for water.

Diogenes came at eight-thirty. After the thawing process had been completed, he cut strips of fiberglass insulation and taped them around the pipes. "You should be all right now, ma'am," he said as he stood at the kitchen sink watching the flowing in and running away. Then he went into the bathroom to check those taps. "Everything is okay in here too."

"I hope so," I replied.

When his plumbing work was done, he sat in the kitchen and volunteered some information about himself. "I'm a carpenter too, but I ain't working right now. You have a lot of finishing up to do. As I said before, I wouldn't soak you too much."

"I will discuss it with my husband, when I go over to the hospital," I told him.

"That suits me okay. I got to get goin' now." After he left, I took Smoky outside for her nightly frolic in the snow. She reveled and rolled in it, while I carried armfuls of logs from the coach house. Overhead, the sky appeared to be illuminated by innumerable electric bulbs, each one blinking with varied intensity. The air was fresh, pine-scented and cold enough to pinch my nostrils. In spite of my warming work, I was forced to hasten indoors, and Smoky came prancing after me.

My usual routine for retiring was unvaried, and as I lay in bed, I could hear the nails in the house contracting with the frost, and the little animals having their supper of vegetables in the cellar. I began planning the next, or the most important, work to be done if Wilmot decided to hire the carpenter. I remembered a poem about work.

> By decreasing the number of things
> We have to do,
> And increasing the number of things
> We don't have to do,
> We finally arrive
> At that blessed state of indolence
> So greatly revered by lazy men;
> So much a desideratum
> In the lives of the diligently dilatory.
> The trouble is,

When there are too many things
Which we don't have to do,
We are at a loss to know
Which one shouldn't be done first,
And so,
We worry ourselves to death doing nothing.

13

Sunday morning I heard voices, and when I looked out the bedroom window, the whole Ferguson family was there shoveling the driveway. They had been working quietly, hoping to surprise me. It was unquestionably the most practical demonstration of neighborliness that one could imagine. Now I would be able to spend the whole afternoon with Wilmot.

When I reached the hospital, I discovered that he had been moved to a private room. I knew what that meant, but I gave no sign of perturbation. He was propped in bed, alert and anxious to hear the minutest details of all that was occurring, about the house, about Smoky, and if I was having any trouble getting to work in the bad weather. We talked about everything.

Then he said, "I haven't heard about the crazy customers for a long time."

I told him about one of the women who had come in the other day. She said, "I've been sick and goin' to the doctor this past two weeks. You know what he asked me?"

I said, "No."

"He asked me, 'Was you ever bedridden?' I laughed and told him, 'Plenty of times, and once in a sleigh.'" All the customers standing around waiting to get checked out roared laughing, and she laughed too.

Another thing I told him: I had called Miss Seigel "Miss Sullivan" by mistake. She said, "I went to a parochial school, but I didn't know it showed that much."

Then we got back to the subject of the versatile tradesman. Wilmot said, "Okay, honey, you better see what he can do. Buy a thousand feet of number-one pine for the kitchen and bathroom floors. He should be able to do that."

Then the doctor came in to examine him, and I said I was ready to leave anyway to get home before dark. "Will you bring Smoky with you next time? I miss her," he said as he kissed me good-bye.

It was after dark when I got home. The roads were plowed and sanded, but the going was slow. Medine and Tony came up for a visit. I told them about the handyman. Tony said he would be happy to come up when the flooring was delivered because someone had to be with Smoky. She wouldn't let the deliverymen in the house.

Monday morning I called and ordered the flooring. It was delivered on Tuesday, and Wednesday morning Diogenes was supposed to come early to get the job done. All day at work I experienced the happy anticipation of having a nice hardwood floor in the kitchen. A floor without knotholes, through which the field mice and other little critters came and went. My disappointment was all the more keen, therefore, when upon returning home that evening, I found only half the floor had been laid in the kitchen. I called Diogenes immediately and asked him why he didn't finish the floor.

"I was hopin' to, but the stove and hot water heater had to be moved, and I couldn't do it alone. I'll bring my wife down tomorrow. She used to work on her father's farm, and got muscles from liftin' milk cans and bales of hay. Movin' that stove and hot water heater will be easy for her."

I had to be content with his explanation, but couldn't help feeling that we were getting off to a bad start. He was only charging $1.50 an hour, but the question was, how many hours would he spend talking a job instead of doing it? What was originally a modest undertaking now threatened to become exorbitant in cost, easily doubling the expenditure for the material. This was learning the "hardwood way" that it is better to have a project contracted for, with price and completion date. Otherwise, one is completely at the mercy of the dilatory and incompetent. The difference between the hardwood floor and the subflooring was only three quarters of an inch, but it was most annoying watching out for, and stepping over, the little ridge.

Morning came, and with it, Diogenes and his muscular spouse. She was dressed like a little girl, with ankle socks, red sneakers, homemade skirt, tight-fitting sweater and her long hair tied back with a shoelace. She walked in and out through the snow to get his tools from the truck. I watched the two workers move the heavy appliances to the new section of the floor. She did most of the lifting, but he did all the panting. A more impressive instance of marital cooperation would be hard to find.

I was about ready to leave, waiting for Tony to come be with Smoky, when the telephone rang. It was a call from the hospital. The nurse said, "I'm sorry to have bad news, but your husband has taken a turn for the worse, and has been placed on the danger list. You won't have to respect hospital rules; come and go at any time."

I thanked her for calling and went out to watch for our driver and Natalie to tell them I had a call from the hospital, and that I was not going in to work. Tony said he would be able to stay most of the day and watch out for things. There wouldn't be anyone in the library until nine o'clock. I called the part-time girl and asked her to work for me. Tony made a fire in the living room because the kitchen stove would be disconnected all day. As soon as I could I left for the hospital.

The work team assured me that when I got home in the evening, things would look different. A truer prediction was never made. Things were not only different on my return home, they were catastrophic. Diogenes had finally laid the kitchen floor, but he didn't remove the kitchen sink in the process, so the flooring was butted against it. Worse carpentry was discovered in the bathroom, from which the toilet had been removed, and was now resting in the front hall.

When I called to inquire the reason for disconnecting the toilet, he told me, "I had to take the toilet out to put the flooring down."

"Why didn't you put it back?" I asked him.

He informed me, "You will have to get a plumber to put it back because it will need a new seal, and a plumber has to do that. You won't need the toilet for a couple of nights." I called the plumber immediately, and he came the next morning. It was a bigger job than anticipated. The new flooring raised the toilet three quarters of an inch and the pipes had to be changed.

CHRISTMAS week, especially Christmas Day, drained me emotionally. I spent most of Christmas Day at the hospital. People from veteran's organizations and the Salvation Army came to visit the patients. They distributed little gifts of socks, handkerchiefs and candy. Medine and Tony invited me to have dinner with them. They had all their family around the tree singing carols. The dinner was beautifully served, but sometimes when one is in such emotional turmoil, it is better to stay home. Then you don't have to worry about being a wet blanket and spoiling other people's enjoyment.

With Christmas over, the decorations taken down, the caroling silenced, I began to feel a little better, mentally at least.

Notes and thank-you letters had to be written. The ones to be answered first were to my childhood friends, the Duders. Under the circumstances, one letter to the whole family would suffice. Margaret and Jessie were my chums since grammar school days and our children had played together when they were growing up. The Duder men, Edwin and Caywood, lived in Long Island, New York, with their widowed mother. Edwin, a poet, was over forty years old. He had just gotten his first job as film editor for Universal Pictures in New York City. Caywood, or Cay, as everyone called him, was an engineer on the New York Central, following in the footsteps of their father who had been a railway executive.

Neither Edwin nor Cay had ever married. When I lived in Somerville, we were together all the time, but since we moved to the country, I hadn't seen them. They could come to East Hartford on the train from Boston, and we could pick them up in Hartford, which was convenient. But there was no way to get out to Canton Center, except by car, and they didn't want to try that in winter.

My friends, Lil and George Hurley, had not been to the country either, and George was used to winter driving. He was a casket salesman, and when he was on a trip to Hartford, he always took Lil with him. They would stay with us for the week, or until he got his orders.

December, with its snowstorms and zero temperatures, gave way to January. I drove my own car when the roads were plowed and sanded, dividing my time between the hospital and library. I wrote a letter to my supervisor explaining my situation. He immediately sent a substitute to stay until I could get back full-time, but she fell on the icy street and broke her ankle. I felt obliged to spend a little more time at work, at least be back late in the afternoon to take care of the people who stopped on their way home, and to close up.

Tony would come up for a couple of hours on his days off

to take Smoky out and bring in logs to have a nice fire going when I got home. They were such wonderful friends. However, the handyman was becoming a handicap. He didn't do anything right. The oil burner was leaking since he moved the stove. I had to keep a bowl under the connection to protect the new floor from oil stains.

One night I received a telephone call from Lil. She said, "George will be in Hartford for a week making calls, I'll come down with him."

I told Diogenes to rent a sanding machine and prepare the seams on the Sheetrock for painting. I wanted the walls nice and smooth, with no tape showing. It had to be done right away, because guests were coming. He said, "Okay, I'll bring Joe to help me. He won't soak you much." I thought, Another one who won't soak me much.

Medine said Tony would be off the next day and would go up to get Smoky, and keep her with them all day. Lil and George were waiting for me in the library parking lot and followed me home. We went into the bedroom and I was appalled at the mess. Instead of preparing and sanding the wall, they opened the can of paint I had unfortunately left in the corner of the room. They painted over the rough wall. They had crushed their cigarette butts out on the floor. They had left their lunch scraps and papers on the floor. They didn't bother to fill the oil jug. The fire was out and the house freezing.

I was on the verge of tears when Lil said, "Don't let it get you down. You have enough to worry about. We'll clean up the mess." Just then Medine and Tony came in with Smoky. They were delighted to meet my old friends. Tony and George took care of the kitchen stove and fireplace. We women cooked and cleaned.

The next day, Lil went with George all day while I went to the hospital and library. She said it would upset her too much to see Wilmot in such pain. She had had several cancer operations during the years, but was at present in what the doctors said was remission. It was a nice visit in spite of the cold house and other annoyances.

When they were leaving, George said, "I'd be afraid for Lil to stay here alone. She might get raped."

14

A lonely woman is a servant of time. Will I get out of work on time? Will I get to the hospital on time? Will I get home in time to fill the oil jug? Will I get home before the store closes? Will I get home in time to feed Smoky?

Time passes quickly in spite of everything. The month of January was drawing to an end. Natalie was not working since the Christmas season was over, so she came down during the day to let Smoky out for a little while to play with their Saint Bernard, Tucker. She also took care of the oil jug. When the pipes froze, she would call Mr. Eustace, and his son Bob, to come over and thaw them out. She also helped me cover around the top of the well with straw to keep the wind and cold from getting through the spaces between the rocks.

Bob suggested that I call Jerry Hartley, a reliable carpenter who lived in Collinsville. Jerry said he would be glad to help, but he was working full-time at the Collins Company and would only have a few spare hours in the evenings and on Sundays. He also said his wife was expecting their fourth child soon, and when the baby was born, he would have to help out at home. But he would see what he could do.

I was with Smoky in the evenings when Jerry worked. He did a nice job of preparing the wall for painting, and he hung the bedroom doors and put trim on the windows. He also installed thirteen feet of shelves on the wall over the kitchen sink. These would be the nucleus for the cabinets. Mary and Frank came out whenever they could. She put dishes on the shelves and did other helpful chores. Then Jerry's wife had the new baby, and construction was again at a standstill. I was grateful for what he did do, though.

When I went to the hospital again, the door to Wilmot's room was shut. I tiptoed in. He didn't notice me. He was in terrible pain, and calling aloud, "Won't someone do something for me? If I were a horse, you would shoot me." I tried to hold him, but he was thrashing around.

I hurried down the hall to the nurse's station. "He's had all the medication we can give him. He will be asleep soon." I asked her if I could see the doctor. She made a telephone call and the doctor came from a nearby office.

He instructed the nurse to give Wilmot another shot. Then he turned to me, "It's up to you, if you want to stay. I can guarantee you, nothing will happen tonight. He will be quiet now. Why don't you go home and come back in the morning." Smoky was in the car, so I said I would leave.

It was cloudy, and the cold penetrating when I left the hospital and went over to the Newmanns' for supper. We were sitting talking when the woman next door came in covered with snow. That was the first inkling we had that a storm was in progress. She said, "It's been snowing about an hour. They say the roads are slippery. Didn't you people have the radio on?"

I started for home immediately. The traffic was bumper to bumper. Cars were slipping and sliding across the streets, no one seemed to be making much headway in getting home. It would be impossible for me to get over Avon Mountain in the storm. As soon as I got to a side street, I turned around without getting stuck in a snowdrift and started back to the New-manns'. When I telephoned Natalie to tell her I couldn't make it home, she said she would fill the oil jug tonight, and again in the morning. She had the Newmanns' number if anything was wrong at the house.

The next morning, I left Smoky with Mary while I went to the hospital. The roads in the city were plowed and sanded, but I was wondering about the country roads. As I walked past the nurse's station the supervisor called to me, "Mrs. MacNeill, the doctor would like to talk to you."

She walked me to his office. The doctor said they were try-ing a new drug, and doing everything possible to keep Wilmot comfortable. "But I think you should notify any relatives. I understand you have two sons." I told him where the boys were. He said, "If I can wire the navy, the Red Cross, or any-thing, I will gladly do it."

I thanked him and said I would take care of everything.

He replied, "Your husband doesn't know if you are here or not. Go home and take care of things."

Wilmot's brother, Jack, and Jack's wife, Neva, came from Saugus, Massachusetts, as soon as they could. The doctor had a talk with the three of us. "The poor chap is sinking. God knows, I wish we could do more. I know it is heartbreaking to watch the one you love dying the agonizing death of cancer."

"Is he unconscious, Doctor?" I asked.

"No. He is heavily sedated." The doctor walked into the room with us. He patted Wilmot's face. "Wake up, Mac, you have company." Wilmot opened his eyes and recognized us. He was surprised to see his brother and Neva. We talked for a few minutes, and then he went back to sleep.

The next day, his relatives had to go back to Saugus, so I went over alone. Wilmot was awake. He remembered the visit of Jack and Neva, and asked when they were coming back. I told him, "They will be back Sunday." He reached out and took my hand.

"I won't be around much longer. I don't want you here watching me when I kick off. You've been through enough. Now listen to what I have to say. Keep a home of your own. Don't go live with the children. As long as you have your own home you will be independent. You have a nice job, and you will get my army pension. Now, remember what I said."

Those were the last words he spoke. Soon he lapsed into a coma, and died.

> *Slowly dims the light of day*
> *Up the hill and far away;*
> *As I labor home to Thee,*
> *God, my father welcomes me;*
> *Long the way has been, and I*
> *Gladly put my grievings by;*
> *Gladly now accept farewells*
> *As the dirge of tolling bells*
> *Startles all who dread to hear*
> *Mortality alarm the air.*

AFTER services in the undertaker's parlor, we went back to the house. The burial would be postponed until spring. The undertaker said, "We can't open the ground in this below-zero weather." A couple of months later, Wilmot was buried without ceremony. I couldn't endure two funerals.

Some thing or some part of my life was gone. I was too numb for grief. I silently watched as brother Bill and Mary packed their things and prepared to leave. Jack and Neva also had to go early. Jack said his eyes were bad, and he didn't like to drive after dark. Bill patted me on the shoulder. "You should come home with us."

Mary agreed. "You could bring Smoky."

George took Lil by the elbow and raised her out of the chair by the hearth. "We have to get going too. There is another storm coming, and I don't have chains with me." Then he turned to me. "You know you are welcome at our house too, if you decide to come to Somerville."

Jack asked, "Whatever possessed the poor chap to buy a place way out here? And in his condition too."

Frank Newmann answered that question. "He was looking for a place in the country for ages. You should have seen how happy he was the day he bought this place."

"We should be going too," said Mary. "Frank has to go to a meeting tonight."

Frank kissed me on the cheek. "We'll call you in the morning and see if you need anything. Will you try and get some rest?"

George was standing in front of the fireplace, with one hand on the mantle. "I'd turn the key in the goddamn door, and get the hell out of here. Better still, I'd put a roaring fire in the grate and leave the screen down. Then turn the key in the door and let the goddamn place burn down."

Two women who lived over on Highway 179, who were good enough to offer to stay to take calls at the house while we were at the service, looked at each other in surprise, and said they had to go home to get supper.

When everyone had left, I took Smoky out for a romp. It was almost dark. I thought,

> *What if the road be rough and long*
> *What if the night comes down too soon,*
> *A taste of wine, and a trill of song,*
> *Can oriole an afternoon.*

Smoky jumped around biting at the snow, tossing the crusted pieces up and running after them. When we went inside, I changed clothes and sat by the fire. I sat there all night wondering, How did I get home alone from the hospital the other night? How did I get through the services without crying? I did remember what the minister and the undertaker said. The burial would have to wait until spring.

By morning I had convinced myself that it would do no good just to sit around. Wilmot's last words to me were "Keep your own home. Don't depend on the children." So, I decided to get the place finished, and have a home of my own.

The telephone rang. It was son Bill calling from California. He said his leave had been granted and that he would start for home. I told him it was all over, and that I would like him to stay in San Diego in the warm weather, not come here to the cold house and snowstorms. I said I would take a trip to see them as soon as I could get things taken care of, when the weather was mild enough, and the pipes wouldn't freeze. He reluctantly agreed. Then I received a call from Tom. He had been on a trip to the Superstition Mountains. I told him the same thing: Stay where you are and I will be out to see you. He felt terrible; all he could say was "Keep your chin up, Mother."

There were several more calls from Massachusetts and New York. All the Duders had been to an aunt's funeral in New Jersey, and they were sorry that they could not be with me. It was Edwin who wrote the next week. He said, "We will be up to see you as soon as the weather gets better. It would be inconvenient to be caught up there in a snowstorm. Keep in touch."

Next came the emotional task of writing to Social Security, the insurance company, Pratt and Whitney, and the British pension commissioner. Wilmot had served in the Scottish army, the Black Watch, and had worked at the Pratt and Whitney aircraft factory in Somerville, Massachusetts. The replies were prompt, but disappointing. From Social Security I was informed, "You are not entitled to your husband's Social Security because there are no children under eighteen years old." The personnel manager from Pratt and Whitney wrote me a letter stating, "We are sorry to inform you that your husband did not contribute to any of our annuity or savings plans. We often approached him about it, but he preferred to do his own banking. Sorry, if there is anything we can do for you, do not hesitate to contact us."

So the only income, besides my own earnings, would be the army pension. I seemed to hear Wilmot's words ringing in my ears: "Aren't you ever going to learn to take care of yourself?" I told myself, You are forty-four years old, the boys are grown and away from home. You will learn to take care of yourself.

15

*W*hen the basic structure of one's life is suddenly demolished, a temptation arises to run away from everything remindful of circumstances and surroundings linked with the catastrophe. There is a strong impulse to put on one's hat, walk out the door and never come back. That is the typical reaction. Like every woman, I cried my tears, and had my moments of despair, but gradually began to reassemble the shattered pieces of a former existence. And so, life goes on. There is little that is admirable in turning one's back on the future.

The storm that had started four days ago continued until the snow piled up to the window ledges, and the car, which was left outside, was buried up to the windshield. I kept a path shoveled from the back door to the coach house. When a young man tapped on the back door, it was a surprise to see someone about.

"Would you like me to plow you out?" he asked. "I just

bought myself a little snowplow, and I'm doing some of the driveways up here."

"Indeed I would," I told him.

When he finished the job, he said, "Too bad you didn't have the car in the coach house out of the storm. I could have done a better job." I told him the snow was so slippery the night the storm started, that even with those doors, I could not get the car in. It kept sliding around from side to side, and I thought it better to leave it out than to bang it into the side of the door. He left smiling and happy with his little business venture.

The feeling of freedom overwhelmed me. I had to get out now. The road was plowed but not yet sanded, so Smoky and I walked up the road. The countryside was like a fairy land, a white world with patches of color peeping through. The red barn down in the pasture. The green roof of a house. The red bricks of Cherry Brook school, looking like a huge fireplace at the end of a long blacktop driveway. The flag waving again at the background of clear, blue sky. The two gas pumps stood like big red tulips in front of the Canton Center store. I didn't intend to walk so far, but everything was so beautiful, I just kept going.

I went into the store to get warm. The people grouped around the potbellied stove patted Smoky and talked to me for a few minutes, offering both sympathy and advice. "Do you have any children?" one woman asked. I told her we had two sons but they couldn't get home at this time. "Never had no kids myself." She shook her head. "My husband is a truck driver and works nights."

The mail jeep pulled up in front of the store, and those who were waiting for seed catalogs and other harbingers of spring moved over to the post office section to wait for the postman to empty the bag and sort its contents.

The walk was both tiring and exhilarating. After a hot meal, I got back to the business at hand and more letter writing. The correspondence was the most depressing task of all. I'd received a letter from Edwin Duder. He said, "Our thoughts are with you, and we will be up to see you in the spring." He included one of his poems.

ABOUT ONE WHO LOVED LIFE

When living,
He loved to lie on the earth,
Gazing up at the sky
Of unclouded blueness,
And with love in his heart,
And a smile on his lips,
He would say;
"Dear Life, I love you so."
Now dead,
The earth he loved
Lies over him,
And over the earth
Skies cloudy and cloudless,
And with love in His heart,
And a smile on His lips,
God says, "I who am life
Love you also."

I went to bed early that night, but tired as I was, I could not get to sleep. The vacant bed next to mine and Wilmot's photo on the mantelpiece directly opposite the beds resurrected the past with unbearable vividness. This is, I am sure, a fairly common occurrence among the recently bereaved. One does not shut out the past as easily as one pulls down the window blind against the darkness of night. It is better to make the memories welcome, and in time they will become visitors to look forward to, rather than intruders to whom we are compelled to accord hospitality.

Sleep finally came, but it was restless and rife with extravagant imaginings. All the light switches were squirrels, and in order to turn them on and off, I had to press firmly on their heads. In the living room, woodchucks and muskrats had trap-doors in the ceilings through which they skittered down chutes in a frenzy of competition. It was all so fantastically matter-of-fact, I was forced to leave my warm bed to investigate. There were no trapdoors in the ceiling, and the light switches were definitely metallic, not mammalian.

I realized that the emotional strain of hard work had finally caught up with me. I needed to take a rest. I would ask for an early vacation and go visit the children in California. I told Medine and Tony the next time they came up. They thought it would be an excellent idea. Medine said, "We will look after the house while you are away. You won't have to worry about pipes freezing now. I'm sure you will take Smoky with you."

When I mentioned my plans to Natalie and Bob, they too thought it would be an excellent idea. Bob said, "You have to get away from it for a while. I'll take care of probating the will, and get the property in a deed in your name. Don't worry about the place, we'll look out for things. Make arrangements for whatever you want to do. Make plans for a vacation as soon as you can."

The next time Mary came in town to have lunch with me, I told her that I was thinking about a vacation, but so much remained to be done in the house, and just the little insurance policy to pay for it. Ambivalence was bothering me.

"How many things? Which is the most important? And what about you? Don't you think you're important?"

I said, "I can't go through another winter without heat. But it would be ridiculous to have a furnace installed until the windows and trim were in upstairs, and a solid hatchway over the stairwell. The ladder would have to be replaced someday with a nice oak stairway. The old cellar doors would have to be repaired, or new ones built. If the house was all warm and comfortable, the amenities could come later."

"I agree with those things," Mary replied, "but what about

you? You're getting too thin." It was time for me to go back to the library. Mary said, "Frank and I will be out soon."

The days were getting longer, with more sun to melt the snow. Lil and George came down on another business trip. She went in town with him in the daytime. She wouldn't stay alone. "Not even with the dog," George said.

We sat around the hearth and talked after supper. Lil thought a vacation was a wonderful idea. She said, "I'll drive out to California with you. While you are in San Diego, I'll stay with Georgie in Torrance. I'll pay half the gasoline expenses, and we will go Dutch on the meals and motel. What about the dog?"

"I'll take Smoky with me."

"Will she be allowed in a motel?" Lil asked.

"She's a lot cleaner than some people I know," I assured her.

George said, "I told you what I would do with the place. Burn the goddamn place down before you go. I wouldn't let a woman live out here in the sticks. What will you do for a social life? Where can you go out here? Not even a movie within twenty miles."

Lil passed him the *Hartford Courant*. "Here, read the paper and I'll make you some hot chocolate."

"How do you get the paper out here?" George asked. "Do you have to go to Avon for it?"

"It's delivered by dogsled," I said. I felt sorry, even embarrassed, to have made such a nasty reply, but there were times when George had a grating effect on my nerves, and when he left for home I needed an anodyne.

My supervisor was most considerate. He arranged for a substitute so I could take the vacation the last two weeks of March and the first of April. I wrote and gave Lil the dates and said I would be ready to drive out at nine in the morning. We would get through New York before the heavy afternoon traffic.

She and George arrived at one o'clock on our takeoff day. He said, "We haven't had lunch yet."

"Neither have I. I've been ready to leave since nine this morning. The refrigerator is cleaned out and everything put away."

"Well, Lil has to do my income tax before she leaves."

"I hope it won't take long, George, because I'm leaving this afternoon." He didn't appreciate that attitude, and they sat at the dining room table working on the papers. She had a lot of the figures ready, but it still took a lot of time. Then he had to transfer all of Lil's baggage to my car. He had boxes and bags of things to bring out to their son, Georgie. The backseat had to be free of bundles and suitcases. That was Smoky's spot. So they fussed and fumed, and finally Lil and I took off for California, and George went back to Somerville. We arrived in New York City right in the five o'clock traffic and it was early evening by the time we pulled into a motel in New Jersey, hungry and tired.

Lil was already feeling pangs of guilt for going away without George. She was always the one who waited at home, always ready at his beck and call. Now she was wondering how he would make out without her.

During the days traveling, and nights in motels, we talked as most women do, about husbands and family. Lil said George was the only man in her life. She never had a date with anyone else. They practically grew up together. She said when they were tots, she pushed George down a flight of stairs and to this day, his mother had never forgiven her.

The trip was pleasant. I took Lil to her son's house in Torrance, and I stayed with my son Bill, his wife, Billie, and granddaughter, Krista. And Tom came over from Phoenix for a visit.

AFTER AN enjoyable vacation with Bill, Billie and Krista, Tom and I started back to Connecticut, each of us in our own car.

Following another car for three thousand miles was an unnerving experience. We stopped several times a day—we needed a break, and so did Smoky. She was wonderful the whole trip. She sat up in her backseat and looked out the window. When we went in a restaurant, we always brought her out an ice cream. Tom took a lot of pictures on the way back. There were so many interesting places to see. Lil decided to stay in Torrance another month, then fly home. She was really enjoying California.

It was late Easter Sunday afternoon as we drove our cars down the ramp of the George Washington Bridge, bumper to bumper with the New York City motorists. I was in the middle lane and could not move right to the Connecticut exit. I tried to nudge over, but the traffic officer forbade me with frantic blasts of his whistle, and waved me on to the metropolis. Tom had already disappeared in the right direction, leaving me to cruise all over Manhattan looking for the Connecticut Turnpike exit. The twilight fingers of darkness were touching the skyscrapers as I aimlessly drove up and down the avenues, wishing I were on foot and could mingle with the style-conscious New Yorkers dressed in their Easter parade finery. Finally, as I stopped at one of the innumerable traffic lights, I saw a Connecticut license plate on a car in the next lane. I called to the driver, "Are you going home? I'm lost."

He hollered back, "Follow me." I edged in behind him as the light changed. When we reached the Connecticut Turnpike, he honked good-bye and sped into the night carrying my blessings with him. It was eleven o'clock when I reached home, and banished a case of nerves to which Tom had fallen victim. He was building up in his mind some terrifying reason for my delay. Smoky raced up and down the back lawn and rolled ecstatically on the ground. Later, I walked down to the brook with her and watched approvingly as she lapped the cool water jeweling over the rocks in the moonlight. Tom and I were too restless to retire. He brought in logs and lit the fire.

We sat by the fireplace, just talking and planning what we would do with the house. So much needed to be done, but the question was, what should be done first?

At eight o'clock the next morning I went down to the Canton Center store. There wasn't one person on the road. A deer and her fawn were nibbling on roadside bushes and didn't seem to notice the noise of the car. Pheasants with their broods were leisurely moving toward the cornfields, and the maple trees arching the road were hung with buckets to catch the sap. It was plainly a pastoral scene that would have delighted the heart of a modern-day Orlando meandering in search of an elusive Rosalind.

That evening Medine and Tony came up to hear firsthand about the trip. A little later, Bob and Natalie dropped in. We sat by the fire and discussed the places we had seen, and the places they had seen, and places we all hoped to see in the future. Tom extolled the climate of Phoenix and proclaimed, "That's where I plan to settle down." Medine had other ideas. She would like to travel, but insisted that the best part of traveling is returning home, and that home was Connecticut, specifically Collinsville, where she had spent many happy years.

Bob and Natalie confided that since they had purchased their property, they had seen no early end to the innumerable alterations that to them were desirable, although not immediately attainable. Much time and money would have to be expended, and at the moment they were long on time but short on cash, "And that," said Bob, "is the long and short of it."

My contribution to the conversation was, naturally, about Krista, the delightful times we had taking her to the zoo, Disneyland, the missions, the desert, on harbor cruises and excursion boat trips. But what she liked best was the section of the Balboa Park Zoo called the Children's Zoo, where the young visitors could pet the animals. Bill's ship had been in port, and he and Billie had come on many day trips with us.

Medine said, "There is no better place than New England in which to live."

Tony concurred. "Nothing could be truer. I hope to go back to my native state of Maine to retire."

All the pleasant chatter continued until the eleven o'clock news. That was when everybody said good night and Medine put her arm around me and said, "It's wonderful to have you home again."

*T*oward the end of May, the colors of spring were gaily omnipresent; the old apple trees, the syringa, lilac, forsythia bushes and wildflowers blossomed and petaled in wild abandon. Around the well, daffodils, crocuses and grape hyacinths formed unbroken circles, and bees airlifted golden freights of nectar to depleted hives. It was an idyllic scene and one from which I reluctantly returned to my own affairs.

Measurements had to be made for the upstairs windows. Tom was already doing so when I finally returned from my communion with the trees and flowers. Together we completed the measuring, and after lunch Tom went down to the lumber company in Collinsville. While he was gone, I went up to the Fergusons' to ask Natalie if she knew someone with a dump truck who would take away some of the accumulated trash. She told me to call Mr. Dainty, the garbage man. When I laughed, she insisted, "That is his real name. Wait until you see the slogan lettered on his truck: 'Do It the Dainty Way.'"

While Tom and I were having supper that night, one of our

neighbors came over from his home on Highway 179. "Just a visit," he said. "I heard you were back."

Then his son came in. "Fine neighbors we are," he declared. "This is the first chance Pa and I had to come over and see you, but we didn't worry, we heard one of your sons was with you. And we knew the pipes wouldn't freeze, the weather was pretty mild." After a few authentic anecdotes about country living and country people, our visitors returned home.

I thought to myself, Life is lovelier in little places. In the cities people pass you by. I said to myself, I will pull myself together. I will get going, and become a part of this friendly community. I realize that there is a certain period of rehabilitation following widowhood during which one must relearn the art of living. It is a difficult time, a time which must not be spent in moody resignation. I am over forty now. It is also a time when one must cultivate a keener interest in the affairs of others, and by doing so, transpose emphasis from self to service. Life can then become livable, and new friends made and kept.

While Tom was at the lumber company he bought an RFD mailbox. It was hard digging the hole, but worth it, he said, because now, if we got home after the Canton Center store was closed, we would have our mail in the box at home. He was in the coach house looking for paint to put the name on the box, and some preservative for the wooden post, when someone honked a car horn. He went out to see who it was.

"Just noticed the new mailbox," said the driver. "You will have to move it. We want them all on the same side of the road. We don't get out of the car."

All Tom could say was "I'll move it tomorrow."

The first piece of mail in the new RFD box was a letter from Edwin. In my last letter to him, I mentioned middle age, readjusting, starting a new life and, as usual, the progress Tom and I were making. He wrote me the following poem.

With forty come the years of complaint;
The double chin
And wrinkled skin,
And a face that wears grotesquely paint.
Then soon, too soon, our hair turns gray;
Our teeth fall out,
And we grow stout,
And all our yearnings die away.

Now is the time when doctors hear
A list of ills
That merit pills;
The sugared kind that cheat and cheer.
And so, our lives continue on
When most of what we were is gone.

I think it is both brave and sporty
For us to linger after forty.

I put the poem away and Tom and Smoky and I took a walk through the woods. One could fish, take long walks, study wildflowers and in a dozen ways be extravagant with time. But, as usual, there were more practical matters competing for attention. While awaiting delivery of the thirteen windows, we gave some thought to decorating the kitchen, something different and distinctive. Tom drove down to Avon and brought back a big book of Sanitas wall-covering samples. We had just settled down to look over the assortment of colors and designs, which challenged our selectivity, when the Raineys from North Canton dropped in to say hello.

Mr. Rainey was a well-known radio personality in Hartford. He had been at station WTIC for twenty-five years. He was also a writer of humorous verse and a purveyor of homespun philosophy, which was just as amusing as it was instructive. The southern drawl in which his comments were packaged and presented did much to make him memorable.

His wife, Odessa, a tall, slender, attractive woman, was at the time employed as a buyer of women's readywear at Brown-Thompson department store in Hartford. Her earnings helped Bud purchase their forty-acre parcel of land with cabin and pond. It was chosen originally for a summer retreat, but they had learned to love it and decided to live in the country year-round.

"I'm forty-five years old now," said Bud, "and I enjoy sitting on a rock with a fishing rod and a few cans of brew."

"To hear him talk, anyone would think he was a dedicated bum," said Odessa.

Tom said to Bud, "You must have a long day; your program comes on at five-thirty in the morning."

"That's right, I do have a long day. I have to leave the house at four in the morning. I used to get home around noon, but since then some joker gave me two piglets and I now have over two hundred. I spend several hours every day collecting food from hotels and hospitals. Those pigs eat the best food in Hartford."

Bud looked at Odessa and said, "Tell the folks what I bought you for your birthday, sugarpuss." Odessa plucked an advertisement from her pocketbook and passed it to me. It bore the picture of something that looked like an inverted washtub, and momentarily I was unable to identify it, until I scanned the text, which boasted, "Here is a cement mixer that is rugged, economical, and priced at only $179.00. It mixes mortar and cement with equal ease. It can be operated manually, or by motor."

Incredulously, I read the text a second time, then looked compassionately at Odessa. "Guess who will be the energizing agent?" she said with a grimace that was almost tearful. Tom advised Odessa to get an electric motor as soon as possible.

"If she doesn't, I will," said Bud. "I don't want a wife with muscles like a weight lifter."

On that amiable note, they rose to leave, but not before Bud made a further contribution to our merriment by exclaiming, "I forgot to tell you, we also have lots of ducks. Someone gave me a pair, and now they're all over the place. Would you like to have some for your brook?"

I said, "Yes, anything but pigs."

After our neighbors departed, Tom and I went back to the wall-covering book. We were now teetering on the brink of decision, and fell over completely when we saw a pattern showing a farm scene with a white background. It had red barns, silos, colonial houses—all sorts of things that would give our kitchen walls the appearance of a rural art gallery. However, we agreed to restrict that particular pattern to three walls. For the wall behind the stove, with the beams going along the ceiling over the wall and down the sides like a picture frame, we would need something plain that would not distract the eye from the beauty of the sanded and polished chestnut.

Our search for the unique was pursued no further than the next week. I was walking through the G. Fox and Company wallpaper department on my lunch hour. At my moment of discovery, the paper was being given special promotion by a representative of its English manufacturer, and a group of onlookers had gathered. Like the others, I was amazed by the appearance of its brick design. Even the mortar protruding from the interstices looked ready for the trowel. It was truly an astonishing example of man's ingenuity.

The following weekend when Medine and Tony came up, Tony, reasonably enough, insisted on touching the wall covering in order to prove to himself that the bricks were not in fact the real thing.

"Seeing is not quite the same thing as believing," he said. We agreed, though not without reminding him that there are some things in this life which must be accepted on faith, especially when they can be neither proven nor disproven.

He was full of news about his activities. He said that the boys at the prison were busy with the Dale Carnegie course, *How to Win Friends and Influence People*. Tony never called the men prisoners, he always referred to them as "the boys." This tidbit of news was told with genuine gravity, not for the humorous effect. He was wholly serious, and went on to say the course would undoubtedly be beneficial to them when they were returned to society. That seemed to be a rational assumption. Nevertheless, it was difficult to smother the thought that such a course, if taken prior to their complicity in crime, might have saved the state a considerable amount of money.

THE UPSTAIRS windows were finally installed. After the carpenters left, Tom and I decided that we deserved a little leisure, and what could be more restful than a stroll along the brook watching our new ducks sail around like miniature gondoliers? They had chosen the deepest part of the brook for their aquatics. What a beautiful spot, with the blue sky, white clouds and trees pictured in the water. The idea hit us simultaneously—what an ideal spot for a swimming hole. The following day, Tom called the steam shovel man. Within a week the pool was deep enough for swimming and diving. The bottom was muddy and not pleasant to stand on, but that was a minor flaw. The deep part would be used for swimmers, the shallow places for nonswimmers, like me, or children.

One hot, sunny day, as I was raking and transporting weeds to a pile in the woods, I noticed that Smoky was having difficulty keeping up with me, and she occasionally sprawled on the grass as though exhausted. I thought the heat was making her tired. Later, when I took her to the store with me, she didn't attempt to get out of the car. When I returned to the house, she didn't even bother to sniff the bundles for some dog biscuits. She lay on the kitchen floor, and I was forced to walk around her as I put things away. This in itself was an ominous sign, for Smoky was not the sort of dog to risk being stepped on. When I finished stocking the shelves, she swayed to her feet to follow me outdoors. It was then that I noticed a puddle of blood on the floor, and that her fur was matted with blood. I coaxed her down to the brook, washed her and looked for a wound. There wasn't even a scratch.

Tom was in West Springfield, Massachusetts, for the day, and when he came home for supper I told him about Smoky. He didn't think there was cause to worry. Nevertheless, enough apprehension remained with me to spoil my attendance at a concert given that evening by "the boys" at Wethersfield prison. My hosts, Medine and Tony, tried to put me in a happier frame of mind by commenting on the appropriateness of a particular solo: "If I had the wings of an angel, O'er these prison walls I would fly . . ." It was no use. My uneasiness persisted. I kept thinking of the sad look on Smoky's face when I patted her good-bye before leaving for the concert. I was being haunted by a premonition that later proved to be well founded.

When I returned home about eleven-thirty, Tom was sitting at the kitchen table, chin cupped in his hands and wearing a worried expression. I felt he had bad news for me.

"Just after you left, Smoky began passing blood, and I rushed her over to the veterinarian in Simsbury. He thinks she may have been poisoned, and he is not sure he can save her." That was bad news indeed, bad enough to keep me awake all night, and when the phone rang at eight o'clock in the morning, I knew before I picked up the receiver that the early caller would be the doctor.

"I'm sorry to tell you, Mrs. MacNeill, that your dog died last night." I thanked him and cradled the receiver, and if my eyes were misty, and my hands shook, who could blame me? I wasn't being overly emotional. I was reacting as calmly as possible to a feeling of deprivation. Smoky had been a dear canine companion, a friend who had shown loyalty and love to her mistress, and never asked for more than a pat on the head and a few kind words. The loss of Smoky was subsequently given added bitterness by the knowledge that she had been, to quote the autopsy report, "a victim of metallic poisoning, presumably arsenic."

When I telephoned this datum to the state trooper, he promised an immediate investigation. "Anyone who would poison an affectionate, gentle dog like Smoky would just as callously destroy a human being," he said. The officer did his best to uncover the culprit, but without success. And so another piece of wrongdoing was added to the incalculable list of man's iniquities.

A couple with two children had recently bought acreage in town and were having a house built. The man came to see me. He said the poisoning of such a beautiful dog had upset everybody in town, especially families with little children, who played in the woods and could pick up anything with poison on it. He said he would write a letter to the *Hartford Courant* about the poisoning. That would warn people to watch out for strangers in town.

Bob Ferguson said, "I'll be glad to start an investigation. If anyone is putting stuff around to kill our pets, the children might get into it. We will post a notice in the post office and store."

The state trooper came to see me. He said he had turned in the report. "Officers in other towns will also be on the lookout for strangers in town who might be dog poisoners. I'll keep in touch."

A friend of Natalie's who lived in Collinsville had a big dog who was annoying the neighbors, and she had to find another home for him. It was the Fourth of July weekend when Tom brought the part-shepherd dog home. He told the woman, "If Bingo bothers anyone, Mother will not keep him." Before Tom left for West Springfield, he said, "I'll stay overnight. You have Bingo to keep you company."

Later, I took Bingo down by the brook for a walk. The Fergusons' dog, Tucker, came charging down through the woods and grabbed Bingo by the throat. Blood squirted from the

wound, and I thought that he would kill Bingo. I got them separated and dragged Bingo back in the house. Tucker followed
and broke through the screen door, and the fight continued.
The blood was all over the kitchen floor, spattered on the
refrigerator, washing machine and cabinets. Tucker dashed
under the kitchen table, lifted it up on his back and tipped it
over, breaking a stack of dishes that I was planning to put on
the shelves. It was a fortunate thing that they didn't go in the
living room, and the cats stayed in the coach house.

Bingo finally broke away from his attacker and crawled
under my bed. Tucker was too big to squeeze in after him.
Natalie told me one day when we were talking about Saint
Bernards that Tucker weighed 210 pounds. I pulled him out
through the hall and kitchen and out the back door, then
closed both screen and inside door. In the confusion I had forgotten to close the inside front door and while I was wiping up
the blood, Tucker came charging through the front screen
door. Again, he tried to get under the bed, and again, I managed to drag him out, and close the inside front door. I wondered afterward why he didn't attack me, and I don't know
how I handled him without getting injured. He was a hundred
pounds heavier than me.

When all the doors were closed, I pushed the bed to the
wall and sat on the floor by the wounded dog. I put an old
shirt under his neck and wiped up the blood. Then I called the
veterinarian in Simsbury. The answering service had him call
me. "How did the dog get injured?" he asked. I told him, and
he said he knew Tucker. "Bring your dog right over. I'll meet
you at the office."

I said, "There is no one to help me carry him. I can't get
him to the car by myself. The Fergusons are away for the holiday weekend and my son is away too. Another thing, I don't
dare open the doors now. Tucker is sitting out there watching."

"Try to get him to swallow three aspirins, that will ease the
pain, and get him over as soon as you can." By this time, Bingo
was in a state of shock. He laid there shaking, and I couldn't

get him to swallow the aspirin. I kept the doors closed, in spite of the heat. Tucker couldn't jump up to get in through the windows, so I kept them open. I kept Bingo's mouth moist by wetting a pad of cotton and dripping the water on his lips. He tried to raise his head, but he was too weak.

When Tom came home, we watched for our chance when Tucker went up the road and we were safe to get Bingo out to the car. His neck had to be stitched. He was at the doctor's place for three days.

Bob and Natalie felt terrible about the incident. Natalie said, "Tucker is a bastard. I'll bet a dollar the poison was intended for him and not Smoky."

Bob agreed and said, "Get the damage repaired and dishes replaced. My insurance will pay for it. We will have to find another home for him."

I felt badly about it too. If I had not taken the male dog on a trial basis, this would not have happened. That was my first experience with animal jealousy. Smoky was a spayed female, and Tucker liked her. My concern now was what to do when we got Bingo back from the veterinarian. The Fergusons ended up giving Tucker away. Later, Natalie said the new owners put him to sleep. I kept Bingo.

By the end of the second summer, the converted barn in Canton Center was becoming a topic of conversation and much interest. I was now referred to as "the widow down by the brook." Two reporters and a photographer from the *Hartford Courant* came out and did a feature story about it for the Sunday magazine section. The photographer emphasized the size of the living room in one photo, and the fireplace wall with floor-to-ceiling bookcases in another, and the kitchen picture was taken from the front hall. It showed a sunny, uncluttered room with excellent counter space and work area. The exterior shot of the front of the house wasn't as inviting, interesting or flattering as the inside one. The camera picked up all the patches, and the new clapboards that were still unpainted. It was too bad they didn't come back later for a picture, when the new roof and siding were installed and the cherry-red shutters hung on all the windows.

Until the new roof, torrential rain leaked through the old, dried-out shingles, and I was kept busy emptying buckets and pans during storms. I called one of the well-known roofing companies in Hartford and made an appointment for a salesman to come out on my next Monday off. He spent two hours talking and measuring and making dire predictions of what would happen if I postponed installing a new roof. He also suggested new sidewalls. The latter had not occurred to me, as the clapboards had been patched and the new boards painted. His selling point was "Painting a house this size will cost you a couple of thousand dollars every five years. That's a lot of dough. If you decide to use our sidewalls, you won't have to put out that much, and you won't have to paint."

I asked him how much it would cost. The figure given was a staggering $1,350 (in 1952, that was a lot of money) and he amended it to $1,300 when he saw my eyebrows raise with incredulity. I said, "I'll have to think it over, and get other estimates too." My decision was obviously unwelcome. His concern for my losing battle against the elements showed a marked decrease and he sulkily took his leave.

Tom was now rooming in Springfield to avoid commuting, and came home weekends. One Sunday we spent the entire afternoon driving around in other towns, noting the color of sidewalls and roofs. We finally decided on weather-beaten gray for the sidewalls, and multicolored shingles for the roof. The house and attached coach house measured seventy-four feet across the front. I suggested cherry-colored red shutters on all the windows, with the front door painted the same cherry color, and solid brass hardware would make the place look cozy.

I made an appointment with another roofing company. Their salesman came out and subjected us to the most obnoxious kind of sales talk. He was relentlessly tiresome about the superior qualities of his product, until Tom remarked irritably, "You don't have to solicit this business, so why do you go through all that rigmarole." This brusque revolt against repetitiveness brought immediate results. He quoted a price that was much higher than the previous estimate. "That's all we want. A price on the job," Tom said. Without hesitancy we both labeled it exorbitant. A stalemate had been met, and looked to be insurmountable, but the man was determined to make a sale and revised the figure to $1,200. That was more like it. I signed the contract with the stipulation that the work be started immediately. That was agreed upon. But, at this point in our contractual relations, I made what is sometimes referred to as an egregious blunder; I failed to insist upon a completion date.

A week later, the company sent out three men. They erected scaffolding and started work on the roof. They completed three courses of shingles and left for another job without saying when they would return. When another week passed by and they failed to appear, I made several inquiries to the office asking the reason for the delay, and the pat and persistent answer was "We're waiting for another shipment of shingles." That seemed to be a peculiar way of doing business. One did not expect a well-known firm to contract for a job, and not have enough material on hand to finish it.

More weeks went by, with more rain coming in, and more resentment accumulated. Finally, I stopped telephoning and drove to Hartford to see the manager. He was polite and promised prompt attention. However, he also advised me that the contract I had signed lacked a completion date. Another month dragged on, a month of delays and for various reasons. Eventually, the ordeal was over. We had a new roof, new siding, and I had learned something about contracts.

Tom was as pleased with the job as I was. He said, "Now if I'm away for a weekend, I won't have to worry about you carrying buckets of water downstairs. I would like to bring Joan down some Sunday and have you meet her. I'll tell you what; why don't you write Edwin and invite him, and his family, and we will make a party of it? If the weather is warm, we could have a cookout." It was settled. I would get a letter in the mail.

The momentous weekend finally arrived, and with it, our guests from New York and Springfield, Massachusetts. Introductions were made and then the business of getting to know one another began. Complete strangers do not become intimate friends at the drop of a cliché. Fortunately for all of us, our facades of formality were soon demolished by sudden bursts of laughter from Joan. She had been listening to some comments on things in general made by Edwin. Evidently he was in good wit and, as usual, shockingly outspoken in his views. Some people appear to be born with an irrepressible sense of humor, and he was one of them. Perhaps this characteristic of his served more than anything else to differentiate him from his brother, Cay, who was six years older and had seen a great deal of the world when he worked on ships in the merchant marine service, before settling down with the railroad. Their favorite recreation was fishing. They had a boat which they kept berthed in Freeport, Long Island.

The cookout was an unqualified success, except for the annoying mosquitoes. The day was beautiful and sunny, with the crispness of autumn in the air. The men enjoyed the natural beauty of the woods and brook. Cay cut a piece of branch from a tree, made a hook from a pin, dug some worms and caught eleven nice-size trout. He was as excited as a boy with a first catch. He brought out the old black iron frying pan from the coach house, made a fire and sang a little sea ditty as he cooked his trout.

The big old milk table was back in use, now as a picnic table. As we finished eating our trout, chicken, hamburger and fresh vegetables, Joan went out to the car and returned with an apple pie. "Mother made this last night. She wanted to contribute something for the get-together."

The men were delighted. "This," said Edwin, "is the way food should be cooked and eaten, with a minimum of labor and a minimum of formality. Then no one becomes too fatigued to eat, nor too fastidious to grapple bare-handed with well-buttered corn."

Needless to say, a great deal of amusing conversation was sandwiched in between mouthfuls of food. There is no better way of learning to know another person than by listening to what he or she has to say. Somewhere in the spate of words you will hear important clues to the speaker's personality. We are pigeonholed by our thinking. The thoughts we think are as identifiable as the clothes we wear.

After the tidying up had been completed, Tom suggested a visit to one of Canton's romantic sites, known to residents as Bridal Tower. He thought it would be interesting to visitors from New York, as well as to Joan. The six of us piled into Edwin's Chrysler and drove up the hill to the little red house that fronted on Barbertown Road. It was built by Abraham Barber in 1779 and looked remarkably sturdy in spite of its age. Considerable time and money had been expended on its preservation. Bridal Tower had been the honeymoon cottage for the twelve families who had occupied it prior to the present owners, Everett and Elsie Eaton of Collinsville, who maintained it, not as a dwelling, but as a monument to serve as a link with the past.

The small house seemed to be huddled around its central chimney. The front door opened into a hall, and directly ahead there were steep, narrow stairs leading to two bedrooms, one at the north end of the house, and one at the south end. As we stood there looking around us, it was not too difficult to visualize, even to hear, generations of feet, young and old, climbing up toward slumberland. Ancient houses have a nostalgic air about them that affects even those seeing them for the first time. We moved slowly from room to room, admiring the unique features of the little red house. The large stone fireplace in the living room had an English oven, but most of the living was done in the large country kitchen. We took another look around, and then returned to the car.

Mrs. Duder said that she remembered the old wooden washtubs and black iron stoves. Joan wondered how women kept house under such conditions, but the men were more interested in the surroundings.

"There must be a lot of hunting up there," Cay said.

Edwin replied, "I wonder if the residents do much bird shooting. There are lots of pheasants in the woods."

We were home in just a short time, sitting at the dining room table having tea and cookies, when a storm started. Loud claps of thunder and vivid flashes of lightning interrupted our chewing and chattering. We looked out the back door. The air was suddenly still, and then we heard sirens. I rushed to the phone and called the Collinsville firehouse. The operator said, "It's the Edgertons' barn, ma'am." We closed windows and doors before we drove up West Road to Highway 179 to the Edgertons'. Other neighbors were similarly motivated, but there was not much anyone could do. The roof had collapsed, and it was a frightening sight with flames consuming fifty tons of newly stored hay. The rain had started, which helped the volunteer firemen save the farmhouse.

We were all talking at once on the way back to the house. Mrs. Duder wondered about the cows. How would the man be able to milk them now when his barn was burned down?

Cay said, "Wasn't it lucky the fire started in the daytime, when the cows were out in the pasture?"

I said, "Mr. Edgerton will probably take the bucket and milk the cows by hand until he can replace the machinery and a new barn is built."

Joan asked, "How long will it take to build such a large barn?"

"In a few weeks," I said, "the neighbors will get together and make plans for a barn raising. Meanwhile, his herd will be cared for by other farmers, if the need arises. Rural areas are among the few remaining environments wherein neighborliness is practiced rather than preached."

Tom said, "I might be able to give them a hand some Sunday."

Edwin was just thinking about all the work involved in such a project. He said, "That's something I'd like to see."

"I'll let you know when they plan the barn raising," I told them.

Our get-together finally came to an end. My guests assured me that it had been an enjoyable visit, and not without excitement. They would all like to come see the barn raising. Edwin insisted that Tom, Joan and I go down to Long Island soon, before the cold weather, and he and Cay would take us out fishing.

As I waved good-bye and watched the two cars drive up the road, I was again alone with my thoughts. And they were happy thoughts. The coming winter would not present the hardships of last year. The house was all closed up now: new roof, new sidewalls, all the windows in upstairs. The next improvement, or necessity, would be a heating system. My work at the library was pleasant, even amusing at times. That was a happy thought, especially on days when the customers got the titles confused. One day a man asked for a copy of *The Big Rear End*. I knew he wasn't trying to be funny. Trying hard to keep a straight face, I said, "You probably want the story about Fanny Brice; it is *Fabulous Fanny*. All the copies are out. I'll call you as soon as one comes back."

A woman wanted "Something that's well written. I ain't got nuttin' to read tonight." I gave her a mystery. She said, "There's nuttin' like a good murder to cheer a person up."

Another day, a minister from the cathedral came in; he asked for *The Cain and Abel Tragedy*. I gave him *The Caine Mutiny*.

The next night Medine and Tony came up, and we talked about the visit of the Duder family, and about Tom getting serious about Joan. Medine said, "Barry and Millie are going to get married, and they want Tom to take the wedding pictures." Barry, Medine and Tony's younger son, was marrying a Catholic girl and they wondered if they should tell him that he was adopted. What records would the priest need? I suggested that they talk to their minister. He knew the family background and was familiar with the circumstances. They agreed.

Tony said, "I just thought of something. There will be a zoning meeting Friday night at the town hall in Collinsville. Will you come with us? Or will Tom be home and want to take you?" I had never attended a zoning meeting, and had no idea of how it would be conducted.

Medine and Tony both started explaining. "The lifelong residents, people whose families have lived here for hundreds of years, don't want zoning. They say they don't want city folk coming out here and telling them what to do." Tony said, "But the new people in town, dubbed by the farmers as young executives, do want zoning. They are worried about the future use of all the farmland in the event a farmer sells or retires. If a young couple saves up enough money to buy ten or more acres, and has a home built and is willing to travel twenty miles each way to work, they want to ensure their privacy. They don't want a builder to get a parcel of land and put houses on acre lots."

Medine said, "We understand the young executives' uneasiness about the growth of the town. But what about the young married people who were born and grew up in town? They have only five or ten acres given to them by the family. Naturally they are worried about wells and septic tanks leaching the fields. With washing machines, dishwashers and two bathrooms in the new houses, there would be a soil problem."

I remembered a conversation I overheard one day at the store, when a woman said to a friend, "No wonder our taxes are going up. These city folks coming out here and wanting indoor plumbing . . ."

The other woman replied, "If a lot of people move out here, they will want a new school."

"Let's forget about the zoning problems and have some tea and nut bread," I suggested.

"No, thanks," said Medine, "we have to get going."

ONE SUNDAY, a couple of weeks later, Tom and I made a trip to Long Island, New York. It was a beautiful day, both fishing-wise and companionwise. As we were leaving for home, I invited our hosts to come to Canton Center the weekend of the barn raising. Mrs. Duder accepted for all three, saying, "Imagine, a group of townspeople getting together to help another farmer build his barn."

On the way home, Tom talked about Joan, his work, his future, and then the conversation got around to me. "You had a good time, didn't you, Mother? I told you to get out and enjoy yourself. You've got to stop comparing people. Your favorite dictum that no man can fill another man's shoes is quite true, but only in the sense that no man can, nor wants to fill another man's shoes. Personalities differ, and it is a fortunate thing for us they do. Take Edwin, for instance; he is burst-ing with personality. He is kind and considerate and full of fun. And Cay is shy, and also kind and loving, but I did notice that they are both completely dominated by their mother. She rules the roost. She treats the men as if they were children. Did you hear her say to Edwin, 'Give me the keys. I'll hang them up so as I will know where they are'?"

I said, "That was the reason Cay left home when he was in his teens. He worked in the merchant marines and did a lot of traveling. When he enlisted in the army, his mother went to the recruiting office and kicked up such a fuss to get him out that she embarrassed the whole family. She told me she 'bought him out.' She said she wouldn't let her son go to war and get killed. It was after that he decided to go to New York City and work on the railway—the New York Central. He lived at the Y for years after that. When his father died and his sisters, Margaret and Jessie, married, Cay invited her and, of course, Edwin to come to New York to live permanently."

"They couldn't all live at the Y," Tom said.

"They rented an apartment on West Fifty-first for a year. In the interim, someone offered Edwin a job as film editor for Universal Pictures, and then they bought the house in Long Island."

"Why wasn't Edwin working before that?" Tom inquired.

"Because his mother said she needed him at home. He took her shopping and to her bridge parties and church activities. She went out every afternoon and some evenings. That is why he didn't finish college. And why he asked for the midnight-to-seven-in-the-morning shift, so he would be free in the afternoons to take her places. She never did learn to drive."

"The poor guy." Tom sighed. We were up as far as the Merritt Parkway and still talking. Tom said, "You've known the family a long time, haven't you, Mother?"

"Since I was a little girl. I attended the same school as Jessie and Margaret. Margaret is my age, and Jessie is two years older. Margaret was a beautiful girl with long blond hair and large blue eyes. She resembled the English side of the family. Jessie was two inches shorter than Margaret, with coal-black hair and brown eyes. Their dispositions are as completely different as their looks: Margaret, reserved and ladylike, and Jessie, full of fun, and always telling outrageous jokes."

The song says, "I could have danced all night." We could have talked all night, but we were tired and hungry and it was after midnight. I said to Tom, "Anything else you would like to know about our friends, I'll tell you next week. And you will have to describe Joan's family to me."

18

The whole story of a woman's life might be summarized in one word—adjustment. She grows up and marries, leaves the family hearth, and moves into a new dimension of living. She is now an adult in an adult world, and must assume the responsibilities of her new status. Then comes motherhood.

One of the emptiest days in a woman's life is when her firstborn enters kindergarten. This is an unavoidable feeling, although one or more brothers and sisters may well keep her mind and hands occupied. Then the years slip by, and such occurrences become routine. Before you know it, the kindergarten has given way to grammar school, which in turn is succeeded by high school, and after that college, wherein one is expected to acquire certain disciplines that supposedly enhance one's chances of adding a little butter to the bread of life. Sometimes the routine is interrupted by service in the armed forces. Then comes the heartbreak of kissing them good-bye as they leave for war in the Pacific, watching for the mailman every day, looking for letters, making daily trips to the Red Cross, looking for news when ships are sunk, the excitement of them coming home on leave, and the loneliness of saying good-bye again.

The adjustment to being alone is a slow process. The loneliest thing about being alone is that you are always the odd one. When you go out with another couple, the husband, or friend, of the other woman always pays for your theater ticket or restaurant check. That makes you feel like a burden to them, financially, that is. Another thing that is upsetting about going out with another couple is you see the other woman with her man, and you selfishly wish you had your husband back. Then, you tell yourself, No, I wouldn't wish him back, he was suffering too much. And then you say you're not going out anymore. But, in a large gathering, the loneliness isn't as keen because there are other women without partners there. I noticed this at Barry and Millie's wedding. There were a number of women there alone, and while Tom was busy taking pictures, I had an enjoyable time.

The best anodyne is keeping busy—going to work every day and becoming involved in current and social events, and small-town activities. The Fergusons were wonderful neighbors and friends. They invited me to parties and gatherings. And as always, Medine and Tony did their best to keep me active. There was another concert in preparation at the Wethersfield prison. Tony asked if I would like to go. When I hesitated in answering, he said, "Medine isn't too anxious to go, but this concert is going to be something special," and he mentioned the famous soprano who was going to sing. "You don't have to be nervous when you see all the guards with guns. They have to watch the fellows in case one tries to slip away in the crowd. The concerts are always well attended, and a prisoner could mingle with the patrons and get out."

I assured him that I would not be afraid. "What are you going to wear?" I asked Medine.

"Something like we wore before, a suit or long-sleeved dress."

The evening of the concert, we arrived early and were escorted through the well-guarded corridors while Tony smiled and acknowledged the cheery greetings. "Hi, Coach." The music and singing were beautiful, but the armed guards standing with loaded guns every few feet along the auditorium walls and on the stage behind the curtain made me feel as uneasy as I had been the previous time. I was almost relieved when the performance was over, and we were on our way home.

"What did you think of it?" Tony asked.

"It must be terrible to be locked up and have guns pointed at you all the time," I replied. "The fellows in the orchestra didn't look like killers or any kind of criminals. I realize it is a maximum-security prison, though, and they must be criminals."

"The sad thing about it is that a great many of the boys are in because they were framed, or because they are taking the rap to protect somebody. Others are being paid by influential parties to take the rap, but some are guilty. It is tragic to see so many young people locked up. Indeed it is." Tony sighed.

Medine asked, "What about the ones you bring home, Tony? You keep them in our house overnight, and when I get up in the morning, they are gone with my purse, the radio, or anything small enough to carry off. What about the boy who stole our Studebaker? Look at all the trouble the boys have caused us."

Tony replied, "Yes, honey, but some of them do come from bad environments, and need help and understanding."

"Why was the soprano dressed in a long gown with high neck and long sleeves?" I asked Tony.

"The regulations require that all female entertainers be completely covered, with no bosoms, no neck, no arms showing, nothing that could aggravate the men prisoners," he replied.

"These last two concerts were given by female entertainers; do they ever have men perform?"

"Not as often as female artists, because the entertainers donate their time, and women give more freely of their time than men do."

We pulled in the driveway a little after ten o'clock, and Bingo and the cats were waiting for us. "How is he doing?" asked Medine. "Are the Fergusons going to get another dog?"

"Bingo is a good watchdog," I told her, "but he is not the lovable dog Smoky was. There are no other males in the neighborhood so he is out all day, but I do keep him in with me at night. Natalie is talking about getting a female collie."

"We have covered every subject now," said Tony. "Let's go."

19

*A*s I looked around the house assessing what needed to be done before another winter set in, I listed a heating system as my number-one priority, storm doors and windows next, and it would be nice to have kitchen cabinets and closet doors. They were a luxury, not a necessity. I talked to Bob Ferguson about getting a small mortgage on the property. He came to the bank with me on my next day off. All the bank president asked was "Is that all you need?" Next I called a heating and plumbing company in Simsbury. I told the owner I was interested in having an oil-fired General Electric heating system installed with baseboard radiation. I wanted all the rooms on the first floor finished, and pipes and rough work done upstairs for future expansion. I would like to have someone come and give me a price.

I said to one of the men, "I didn't get your name, Mr. . . ."

"Didn't tell you," he replied, "but it's Darling, Elwyn Darling. Just call me Darling. Everyone does." Then he continued, "I hear John Dunne did the bathroom for you."

"Yes, he did a nice job." Darling looked at me smiling.

"I had a friend who bought a bathtub once and he called me to take a look at it. He said he couldn't use it. When I asked him why, he said he leaned back in it and the taps hurt his head. I thought I'd bust a gut laughing. 'You ain't supposed to put your head in that end, stupid. That's where your feet goes.' He uses it nearly every week now, especially in the summer."

I was having a hard time trying not to "bust a gut" too. I said, "Please tell your boss to start the job as soon as possible. I'm home Sundays and Mondays."

When my friends came for the barn raising, I had the baseboard heating installed, storm windows and combination storm doors installed, and doors on the kitchen cabinets waiting to be painted. It was really beginning to look like home.

Mrs. Duder had her fur coat in the car. She said she expected it to be bitter cold in the woods this time of year. The men wore jackets. It was a beautiful, sunny day. After a quick snack, we drove to the Edgerton farm. Most of the black debris had been removed. We watched a battalion of busy people sawing, hammering, all having a good time as they hollered back and forth, giving orders and asking for helpers. For Mrs. Duder, it was an almost incredible demonstration of what willing hands and good hearts can accomplish.

She kept exclaiming, "Isn't it wonderful."

And just as often I reminded her, "People around here don't think they are doing something extraordinary. It is their way of perpetuating an old colonial custom of pitching in to help when help is needed. Mr. Edgerton will only have to pay for the material."

Cay and Edwin listened to my explanation of what was going on. Cay said, "I hope he has enough insurance to pay for the machinery that was ruined."

We were there only as spectators and took no active part in the proceedings. Nevertheless, we could not escape a feeling of participation. After all, even those who merely stand and watch admiringly do contribute a certain amount of moral support.

The women of Cawasa Grange, a group of farmers' wives who held community fund-raisers, were there in force preparing hearty meals for the workers. As we watched them busily cooking a variety of edibles, it was not too difficult to envision earlier settlers and similar gatherings.

We had a pleasant time. It was too bad that Tom had to work that weekend. He would have enjoyed taking pictures of a barn raising.

After supper, as they were leaving for home, Mrs. Duder said, "Never in my life did I see anything like that. I must write to Margaret and Jessie and tell them about it."

Cay hugged me and said, "I don't know if we will be up again before the snow flies. It must be rough driving up here in winter."

Edwin whispered, "I'll get up alone one day."

20

*A*utumn passed quickly into the white anonymity of winter, leaving the large evergreens with branches spread like wings of a mother hen over the brooding earth. At the edge of the front lawn, a row of blue spruce stood poised like skaters at the Ice Capades. Seen through the bluish haze of moonlight, they had an animated appearance, and momentarily one expected to see them go whirling across the glistening snow. The longer I looked out the window, the more I saw, and the most fascinating sight of all was my nightly visitor, the small red fox. He had become almost domesticated since I started putting out a dish of cat food for him each night. Even wild animals learn in time to distinguish between friends and foes.

From such relaxing moments it was hard to return to making plans for the forthcoming wedding. Tom and Joan had picked the last week in February for the date, and Bermuda for the honeymoon trip. I had to shop for an outfit that was not too juvenile and not too mature. When one is in her mid-forties, that presents a problem. After weeks of looking on days off and lunch hours, I found the right dress and accessories in a specialty shop on Pratt Street. It was pale blue silk organza, not cut too low. It had a boat neckline and cap sleeves. Unfortunately, it was size 14, but the fitter assured me she could take it in without spoiling the lines, and make it a size 12. While she was pinning the dress, two salesgirls picked out a hat, gloves, bag and white sandals. I was delighted that the bride's mother had chosen beige for her outfit, leaving me free to buy blue.

Joan's mother made elaborate arrangements for a hotel ballroom, orchestra, flowers, church, etc. It was Tom's suggestion that Edwin accompany me and sit at the head table with me. There was a little fuss and confusion over this. The people in charge of the wedding arrangements said it wasn't proper protocol, because he was not a member of the family.

The happy Saturday morning dawned with a clear blue sky and a mild breeze. Medine and Tony took some of our friends in their car. Bob and Natalie picked up our new neighbors across the brook. As they drove out the driveway, Edwin and family arrived from New York. It was excellent timing. They said the ride up had been pleasant with not too much traffic. "That's because I suggested an early start," bragged Edwin, "and also because I sang a brand-new poem that could be a song as we drove along."

"Let me hear it," I asked, and was not surprised to hear his latest effusion trembling forth.

> *"Here I come on wings of song,*
> *Nothing to do my whole life long*
> *But sing and sing to the open sky,*
> *And keep on singing till I die,*
> *And you who hear, and you who see,*
> *Would you like to sing as well as me?*
> *Why not, Nightingale, I too was made*
> *To lilt in lyrics, or serenade*

A woman's heart, or rising moon
With voice and flute, and many a tune,
And you who hear, and you who see,
Can you compete in song with me?"

Almost before he had completed his recital, his mother inquired, "Where is the happy bridegroom?" I told her that Tom and his best man, Bill Dunne, and two friends from college had already left for West Springfield, and that Tom and I had been up since six o'clock.

"It's a wonder he went to bed at all in the midst of such excitement," observed Margaret.

Edwin's other sister, Jessie, capped this observation with one of her own. "Have you ever seen a bridegroom who was cool, calm and collected?"

Her innocent query drew Edwin's smiling comment, "He may not be cool and calm, but he has certainly been collected."

This was not, of course, a particularly funny remark, but Edwin had a weakness for the obvious, and sometimes had been known to pillory some perfectly innocuous faux pas. As a rule, however, he managed to curb the wicked impulse.

Tom was disappointed that his Uncle Bill and Mary could not attend the wedding, for Bill was out of town at a company meeting. Lil and George couldn't attend either. George was on the road, and Lil didn't have a driver's license.

Like all weddings, it was a happy affair, full of laughter and the promise of happy years to come. Like all weddings, it was also a little sad, marking as it did the separation between mother and son, which had been anticipated and was now an accomplished fact. Joan's mother said, "When the kids leave the nest they rarely come home to roost." Perhaps that is why most weddings seem to be sad-glad spectacles of conflicting emotions.

Joan looked radiant in her gown of white velvet with train.

The bridesmaids wore pastel shades of taffeta. The mother of the bride looked charming in her gown of beige silk, a shade that enhanced her auburn hair and delicate complexion.

From the church we followed the group to the hotel for the dinner and reception. It was a sumptuous affair, as such things usually are. By late afternoon, after hours of dancing and exchanging toasts, the bridesmaids accompanied the bride to the room upstairs to help her change into traveling clothes. Shortly afterward, she returned to join in the chorus of good-byes as she and her groom were driven to the Bradley International Airport to catch their flight to Bermuda.

After so much excitement it was a relief to return home, sit by the fire and have tea. We merely wanted to simmer down, to become earthbound again after our cloud-borne excursion into the land of romance. That's easier said than done, and Mrs. Duder proved it when she suddenly announced, "I suppose I'll be losing my son one of these days." She was looking straight at me as she spoke.

It was then that Jessie, with her irrepressible wit, lightened the atmosphere. Looking toward her mother, she said, "Give him time, Mom. He's only forty years old."

Margaret smiled. "Good, we'll have another wedding to get dressed for." Another wedding, I thought, as I looked at the three women. The mother had enjoyed many happy years with a wonderful husband. She must have missed him terribly. Jessie married young and had one child. When Jessie divorced, her mother raised the baby. Margaret was divorced and had been keeping company with a man for years, but no signs of wedding bells there. Why had the men never married? Were they inhibited by their mother? Did they think they would be bossed around by a woman, treated like servants, told what to do and when to do it? Two handsome men who did not have dates nor ever brought a woman home with them for Sunday dinner or even a visit with their mother.

I did notice that Edwin was becoming a little more independent and not catering to his mother as much as usual. She complained one day about me "having too many cats underfoot."

Edwin said to her, "Mom, it's Mary's house, and she loves animals."

"Where's the big black police dog?" Margaret asked.

"Bingo went out one night and didn't come back. I'm thinking about getting another dog."

She replied, "Well, it's just as well he went away. I didn't like him."

After everyone left, I said to myself, "It's not so bad living alone."

21

The house was empty again. The cats and I were sitting by the fire. I had a great deal to think about and my thinking had to exclude the past. I had to decide that to be truly alive, one must live with the future, which, as we know, is an hourly occurrence, or to be more accurate, something that happens to us every headlong second. This is a thought that rarely visits the young, and certainly not a pair of honeymooners. It was with some reluctance that I left the warmth and cheer of the fireplace and prepared for bed. I disliked putting an official end to what had been a day of gaiety and romance, of smiles and tears.

Monday morning, while I was having my tea and toast, someone knocked on the back door. It was our new neighbor, Jane Goedeke, with a couple of little ones. She and her husband, Mark, were in the process of building their new home on ten acres, almost across the road from the Fergusons' driveway.

She smiled. "I thought you might be home this morning. You don't have to work Mondays now, do you?"

"No, but there is talk about keeping the stores open six days a week the year round. When the stores are open Mondays, the library will be open. The merchants think, or probably it is the chamber of commerce that thinks the New York discount firms who have opened stores on Main Street might wean away the customers from the old, established, family-owned businesses. G. Fox is still operated by the family. Mrs. Auerback is at the store every day. Mr. Allen is at Sage-Allen every day. Mr. Wise, at Wise-Smith, still goes into the store every day, and he is over ninety years old. They say, 'We cater to the carriage trade. We give our customers personal service. We have generations of the same family dealing with us. We should not have to worry about discount houses. They will have their own type of customers. We should only be open on Mondays during the Christmas season.'"

"I agree with that," said Jane. "People have only so much money to spend, and it seems that five days a week should be enough time to buy what they want."

"Have some breakfast with me," I invited.

"No, thank you. I just finished eating before I came out. I wanted to tell you about the Fireman's Ball. It is sponsored by the volunteer fire department. They are trying to get enough money to buy a fire engine."

"What are they using now?" I inquired.

"An old truck with a pump on it. It's lucky we don't have many fires in town. Edgerton's barn was the only fire in years. That's what people tell us."

"You enjoy it out here, don't you?"

"We love it." She smiled again. "The kids can walk to Cherry Brook School, and we can have animals, and we are planning a vegetable garden in the spring."

Jane's son and his friend were getting impatient waiting for her. The inside door was open and the boys were leaning against the wall next to the glass storm door. They were giggling about something. We heard one of the boys say, "Are you going to Sunday school this week?"

"Yes," replied the other. Then there was more giggling as if they were sharing some big secret. "I told you I was going. I didn't say my prayers for three nights. God will think I'm dead."

"Out of the mouths of children," said Jane as she walked toward the door. "You and your friends will come, won't you?"

"We will be looking forward to it," I assured her. She started to walk away, then turned back. "Oh, I have something funny to tell you," she said as she came back in the kitchen.

"I went into Hartford Saturday to the Y for my ceramic class. I was working next to an English girl. I asked her what she was making. The girl, without changing expression on her face, replied, 'Intercourse ashtrays.'" Jane laughed until the tears rolled down her cheeks and continued. "I asked the girl, 'For pity sakes, what are they?' She told me, 'In England, we don't have as many cigarettes as you do here, so we don't waste them. Between the courses of our meals, we have a little smoke, so we call these little saucers intercourse ashtrays.'" I laughed, and she continued, "I knew you would get a kick out of that." She waved good-bye and walked the kids to school.

Early that afternoon I was busy tidying up the house and getting clothes ready for the week, when the telephone rang. It was my friend Nancy from East Hartford. She said, "Mary, I'm going out to Avon this afternoon to buy some fabric for draperies, and I was wondering if you are going to be home. There is something on my mind, and it is eating my heart out, day and night. I have to talk to someone. You have been through so much, perhaps you can help me come to a decision." I suggested that she come right away. The days got dark early at that time of year.

I put some logs on the fire and a quick, cake-mix cake in the oven. From the sound of Nancy's voice, I knew we were in for a long discussion. In less than an hour she was at the door. She was surprised to see how much had been done to the house. I poured the tea and brought in the hot cake. As we sat at the dining table, she said, "This is a long story."

"Tell me about it."

"I don't want to bore you, and I don't know where to start."

"Start at the beginning," I told her.

"I really don't know how to put it," she began. "I can't tell anyone about it. I don't want to shame Kathy. She is not my daughter. She is adopted. And now she is going to get married. Should she know about her background? I just don't know what to do. Harold says I have to make the decision. He adopted the girls legally when we got married. She thinks Louise is her real sister."

"Have more tea and relax. I'm sure everything will work out. You might not have to tell her."

"I know you are going to find this hard to believe." She sighed. "My first husband and I were married five years when my father-in-law died. He didn't leave much, after all the hospital and doctor bills were paid. My mother-in-law needed help, financial help, that is. It was a case of her coming to live with us, or Joe keeping her in her own apartment. His mother was a stubborn and headstrong woman. I knew if she came to live with us, we would all be unhappy. Joe and I had a serious talk, and agreed that he would maintain the apartment for his mother and I would go back to work for my old boss, Dr. White. Well, everything was going along fine—we were getting accustomed to our new routine. I would bring our daughter to Mrs. Pine in the morning, and pick her up after work. Joe was a schoolteacher, and there were times when he stayed late to correct papers, and there were times when he was quiet. I thought he was upset over the change in our living pattern.

"Well, one day I didn't feel well. Dr. White said to me, 'Why don't you go home at lunchtime? We don't have any appointments this afternoon.' I went in the house quietly, not

expecting anybody to be home. When I walked into the bedroom to change my clothes I almost fainted with the shock.
There in bed with my husband was another woman and her
newborn infant. He jumped out of bed and grabbed me by the
arm. 'Don't touch her, she is awfully sick. Some fever or infec-
tion. I brought her home because I didn't know what else to
do.' 'The baby?' I asked him. He was almost crying. 'The baby
is healthy. She is a week old.'

"I told myself I must be dreaming. I must be imagining
things. I telephoned Dr. White. I told him that my husband
had brought home his mistress and a newborn baby. They
were in our bed. And the woman was ill. He couldn't figure
out what was going on and said, 'Don't do or say anything
until I get out there. I'll leave the office right away.'

"When the doctor walked in, I was almost in a state of collapse. He gave me a pill and a drink of water. Then I went
with him into the bedroom, while my husband stayed in the
kitchen. 'It's a good thing you didn't try to take care of her
yourself,' said Dr. White. 'She has blood poisoning, and this
baby has been neglected since the birth. Where was the baby
born?' I shook my head and the woman didn't move. She was
too weak to know or care what was going on. The doctor
called for an ambulance and the woman was taken to Hartford Hospital. I didn't even ask her name. Dr. White asked,
'What will happen to the infant? Should I call a policewoman
to come and take it?' 'No,' I replied, 'I'll take the baby.'

"Well, to make a long story . . ." She was crying now. It was
difficult for her to talk about it, even now after all these years.

"What did your husband do?" I asked.

"He went in the ambulance with the woman. I told him
never to come back. I kept the baby."

"What happened to the woman?" I asked.

"She died."

"And your husband?"

"I divorced him." She sighed again. "He died of a heart
attack two years later. He never came to see the baby. I loved

him so much, I would have let him come and visit with her. I loved the baby like my own child, because she was his. Now she is a young woman and planning to get married. I don't know if I should tell her the whole rotten story and spoil her wedding. What would you do?"

"I wouldn't know what to do." I shook my head and said, "I really don't know what to say. I would like to call the minister down here at the Congregational Church and ask him if he has a few minutes to spare, if he could possibly advise you."

I called the parsonage, and the minister's wife answered. "He is over at the store waiting for the mail to come in. I'll have him call you as soon as he gets back, Mary."

Nancy was feeling more relaxed now, but I could see that she was shaken from reliving the whole scene. I was nervous about her driving home. The phone rang and after I talked to the minister, she assured me that she was okay and would be happy to stop in and have a talk with Mr. Angell. She would call later and tell me what her decision was.

While eating supper that night, I couldn't help wondering whether Harold knew of Nancy's heartbreak in her first marriage. He had adopted the two little girls soon after they were married. He loved them and he was a good husband to her. But, deep down in her heart, Nancy was still in love with her first, no-good husband. There is no way of explaining a woman's emotions. The day that started out in an amusing way came to a close on a depressing note. Hearing about another woman's inner turmoil can be emotionally infectious.

22

*W*inter ambled into spring, the joyful time of the year when everything is emerging from its long winter nap. With patience, one could watch the petaling of wildflowers, and the butterflies metamorphosing from their mummylike cocoons. It was a time to sit by the brook and meditate or sing.

> *It is spring,*
> *The slapped-bottom*
> *Of a newborn season,*
> *And soon we'll hear*
> *The first, shrill cries,*
> *The fretful mewling*
> *Of infant days;*
> *While the green thumb*
> *Of the year*
> *Fingerprints our gardens*
> *With ever-recurring*
> *Whorls of life.*

As I was driving up the road one day, I stopped to talk to a young dairy farmer. He was removing buckets from the maple trees and dumping the sap into a large container on his truck.

"Good morning," he smiled.

"Hello, Mr. Dewey. Those are beautiful trees. What is the ratio? How much sap do you need to gather to produce a gallon of syrup?"

"It is forty to one. It takes forty gallons of raw sap to boil down to one gallon of syrup. There is a story about these trees. Would you like to hear it?"

"Indeed I would," I replied.

"But first, tell me how you are getting along down at the barn?"

"I'm doing fine. The house is warm and comfortable. I have made nice friends in town, have relatives from the Boston area, and friends from New York come to visit. And my son and his wife come as often as they can, depending on the weather."

"I read the article about your house, the converted barn, in the Sunday *Hartford Courant*. Who would have ever believed it, the old Dean barn made into a colonial home."

"Will you tell me about the trees?" I asked him.

"It seems in the early 1800s, somewhere between 1820 and 1830, a grandson of one of the earlier settlers in town was known to be gifted with hypnotic power, as well as having above normal intelligence. His parents sent him to Albany, New York, to college. After he returned home, he found that farming had lost its appeal, and he decided to go to Texas for a more adventurous life. That huge state was then under the rule of Spain, and Napoleonic law prevailed. Before leaving home, the boy said, 'I'll plant a row of trees and, if I don't come back, they'll be a memorial to me.' In those days, people were tree-conscious, and he was no exception. He went up the mountain and dug a sack full of seedlings and planted them alongside the road. Then he set out for Texas. Almost a year passed and not a word was heard from him until finally, one day, news that he was in trouble reached his parents. As the story goes, he had attended an exclusive party one night, and during the lull between dances, the subject of hypnosis was heatedly discussed. Some claimed that it was a lot of nonsense, and others that it was genuine and accepted by scientists. In order to settle the argument, he offered to hypnotize one of the group. A beautiful young woman volunteered, and in no time at all he put her into a deep trance, but before she came out of it, she died. Her heartbroken father called the police. The unfortunate youth was cast in prison, charged with murder and executed."

"What a terrible thing to have happened. And the trees are still here."

"You know the old saying, Truth is stranger than fiction." He sighed as he went back to his maple syrup cans.

"How many acres do you own, Mr. Dewey?"

"Call me Carl," he said and continued, "I don't own the farm. I rent it from a doctor in West Hartford. He doesn't want to sell the land, and I can't buy much now. I want to get the herd built up first. So, the arrangement works fine for both of us."

"I have to get going. Thank you for telling me about the trees. I'll think of that every time I go up and down the road. So long."

When I got home, there was a letter from Edwin. He was getting a little more courageous in his writing. He talked at length about marriage among middle-aged people—oldsters, he called them. He enclosed a poem as usual.

> *Men who have been know to tarry*
> *Cautious years before they marry*
> *Should let some widow on their list*
> *Divulge to them what they have missed.*
>
> *And if they hear what I have heard*
> *They will not think these lines absurd;*

They will instead, rush out to buy
A double bed, the same as I.
But not, of course, until they find
A widow with a lenient mind
Who'll gladly share what she has got
As soon as the parson ties the knot.

He is getting serious, too serious, I thought. I'm sure I could never remarry. Tom always said, "You've got to stop comparing people, mother. No two people are alike. You have to accept people on their own merits. Stop comparing. You didn't want to get another dog for the same reason. You were looking for another Smoky."

I went around the house doing the work and thinking about Edwin's letter. I convinced myself that I would never get married again. I was used to living alone now. I could come and go as I pleased, go to bed when I felt like it, get up when I felt like it, eat what I liked, when I liked, buy what I liked. The only thing about that was, when I bought something there was no one to admire it when I brought it home. But I talked myself into thinking that I was better off alone.

I looked out the window before going to bed, and noticed lights in the woods down by the brook. At first I thought they were shooting stars. I went in the living room and looked out one of the side windows. The lights were moving around, but I couldn't hear a sound, not a twig snap nor a branch squeak. There was no sound of footsteps because the ground in the woods was still covered with snow. I switched the kitchen light off and looked out the window. The lights were still moving around. They looked like lanterns. I wondered if someone was lost in the woods, or if an animal was missing from a farm. Just then I heard a loud noise coming from the side of the coach house. I looked over in that direction and saw two raccoons running toward the brook. Evidently they had dropped the trash can covers in their nightly search for food. I watched a few more minutes, while trying to decide what to do. Go to bed and forget about whatever was going on in the woods or call the state trooper. I decided to call an officer, but unfortunately, I did not get the pleasant young trooper who came to the house that stormy night when the pipes were frozen. This fellow sounded curt and bored, as if he didn't want to be bothered.

"Stay inside and keep your dog in. I'm not going in the Canton hills tonight. The game warden in New Hartford got shot and badly wounded last week. Those fellows in your woods are jacking deer. Make believe you don't know they are there and they won't bother you."

"I'm here alone," I stammered.

"I said, keep your dog in and you will be all right."

"I don't have a dog now."

"Put all your lights out and go to bed," he replied.

"What does deer jacking mean?" I timidly asked.

"They blind the deer with lights and stab them and drag the carcass off to their truck. If they used a rifle, people would hear them. Just put your lights out and go to bed. Good night."

"Good night," I said to myself. I left the lights on and made some tea and watched the eleven o'clock news, then went to bed, but not to sleep.

> *Ah sleep, that knits*
> *The raveled sleeve of care*
> *If I could sing*
> *As sweetly as Shakespeare,*
> *What lovely songs*
> *Would all the valley fill,*
> *What rosy dawns*
> *Salute the highest hill,*
> *And I awake*
> *To hear the minstrelsy*
> *Of birds foregathered*
> *On a willow tree.*

23

The weekend of the Fireman's Ball was upon us. On a beautiful Saturday at noon, Edwin, his mother and Margaret arrived. "Here we are, ready for the big night," said Edwin. He took his mother's overnight bag out of the car and passed it to Margaret.

"My, the woods smell lovely. It's like walking through the perfume department at Macy's," said Mrs. Duder as she stooped to pick a jonquil.

Margaret said, "Wait till you see the gown I bought at Lord and Taylor's. I hope it is not too elegant for a country affair. What are you going to wear?"

"The dress I bought for Tom's wedding," I replied. Then I suggested, "While we are discussing our finery, let's go inside and have some lunch. You must be hungry after the long ride up."

As the women walked ahead of us toward the house, Edwin took my hand. "One of these days, I'm going to get up here alone for a visit. I want to have a serious talk with you."

"How are you going to manage that?" I asked.

"I'll send Mom to Boston to visit the girls," he replied.

After lunch we women went down to the Canton Center store, where there was a flurry of activity. I asked Tom Leahy, the owner, "What's going on?"

"Oh, I thought you knew about the barbecue, or I would have phoned you. It's a chicken barbecue put on by the women of the Grange. The first sitting is at five o'clock." Some of the men were putting finishing touches on the picnic tables and the cooks were assembling huge grills.

Mrs. Duder was surprised. "What will they think of next?" she exclaimed, "eating your dinner on the street."

Margaret laughed. "I think it would be great to eat here at five o'clock, then we wouldn't have to cook and wash dishes before we went to the dance, or ball, whatever it is. Let's tell the cook we will be back with another person, to put our names down for four dinners."

Just then one of the wealthy men in town got out of his car and walked toward us. "Hello, Mrs. MacNeill, I see you have family with you."

"No, Miles, not my family, friends from Boston and New York." I introduced him to the women.

He shook hands heartily with Margaret. "Is your husband with you, Mrs. Murphy?"

"I don't have a husband," she replied.

"I'm a widower. There's a dance in Simsbury tonight; would you people like to be my guests?"

"Thank you," Margaret replied, "but my brother is taking us."

"Good. I hope I have the pleasure of dancing with you," he said and drove away.

Edwin's mother was amazed at the barbecue. "Wait till I tell Caywood that we ate our dinner in a parking lot between a store and a church, listening to the choir practicing and a funeral going on in the graveyard across the road from us. God knows what we'll be doing next. It's not like the old days, when we got dressed in silks and went to the church garden party."

Edwin laughed. "Think of the fun you're having, Mom."

We drove over to Simsbury early in the evening. I took my car. I wanted to get an easy parking spot so I could leave without maneuvering too much in the dark. Margaret looked gorgeous in her pale pink gown. Her blond hair was done in the new upsweep style. Edwin's mother wore a black-flowered dress and a white ermine jacket. We were seated at a table near the orchestra, which was too noisy. When the dancing started, Miles Fletcher came over and put his hand out to Margaret. Then Jack Campbell stopped at our table. He told Margaret that she looked like a movie star. I danced with Bob Ferguson and our new neighbor up the road. Edwin did not dance. "This is the first dance I ever attended," he told our friends. He sat and sipped punch, which was being added to continuously from flasks taken from men's pockets. Mrs. Duder even enjoyed a couple of dances.

As the evening wore on, the soprano sang more loudly, the dancers danced more vigorously and the tellers of anecdotes laughed more raucously. One neighbor told Mrs. Duder and Margaret about an incident that happened in town not long ago. "One of the businessmen in town was having trouble in his marriage. He went home one night, walked into the bedroom and was flabbergasted to see the room divided into two rooms. (It was a big room originally.) While the husband was away, his wife hired a carpenter to install a knotty-pine wall dividing the bedroom into two rooms—his and hers. I ought to know, I'm the carpenter who did the job." I had already heard the story and wondered why she had their bedroom divided when it was a ten-room house. Why not move into another bedroom or have the husband move to another room? That is the way in small towns; one only hears one side of the story. Bruce Lindsay came over to our table and refilled

Edwin's glass. I got up to waltz with Harry Humphrey, a neighbor over on Highway 179. It was a relief to move away from the singing, which was becoming louder than the music.

When I came back to the table, everyone was laughing heartily. Edwin was holding his face on his fist and his mother was wiping her eyes with a handkerchief. Margaret said, "Tell Mary." He repeated the story about a farm worker who got bored with his chore of peeling bushels of apples every night to make applesauce. He was determined to turn his mistress against it. So one night he caught a large rat and laid it in the stone crock across the top of the applesauce. When she found it in the morning, she got sick. She didn't want any more applesauce. The farm hand scraped off the top of the apple-sauce and ate it himself all the rest of the year. I didn't think that story as amusing as the one about the bedroom. I also wondered how a rat could stay on top of the applesauce. It must have been a lot thicker than the sauce we buy in cans.

"Have you people seen Bridal Tower?" Miles asked.

"Yes," replied Mrs. Duder. "I think it is an interesting place. What fascinated me about the old house is the door at the side of the house. Someone told us that it is the 'funeral door.' Because of the narrow front hall, they could not get the casket out the front door, so they put a wider door in the front side room."

"What amused me," said Margaret, "is the borning room. Can you imagine babies being born in a room right off the kitchen? There wouldn't be much privacy."

"There we go," said Edwin, "from walls down the middle of the bedroom to rats in the applesauce and funeral doors and now borning rooms." He took another sip of his punch and laughed heartily.

I said, "I was amazed at the cupboards at each side of the mantels. Someone told me that was where the farmers kept their gunpowder dry."

"How are you enjoying yourself?" Bruce Lindsay asked Mrs. Duder.

"I'm having a jolly time," she said, "but I didn't expect it to last so long. I thought people in the country went to bed early."

"They will be breaking up soon. The farmers have to milk their cows at five o'clock in the morning."

"I thought they were milked late afternoon," Mrs. Duder said. "I saw the man on West Road getting his cows across the road one day about five or six o'clock when we were coming back from the store."

"They milk them twice a day," replied Bruce.

Edwin, who was feeling bored by this time, said, "The poor cows; no wonder they have a long face."

"This punch isn't agreeing with Edwin," said his mother. "He's getting a little green around the gills. We better go."

"Okay, Mom," said Margaret. We started to help Edwin to his feet. Margaret looked at Miles. "They must have raised a lot of money towards the fire engine. There were a lot of people here."

"I would like to take you down to the Collins Company Museum sometime and show you their old hand pump engine. They also have the first piano that was in town. Perhaps the next time you come up."

"I would love to go with you."

"Will you let me know the next time you are coming up so I will be home that day?"

"Okay," said Margaret.

Edwin's head was beginning to slip off his hand. His eyes were closing. Margaret whispered, "Ed is drunk." Her mother heard what she whispered, and said, "Oh, no, girl, he's just a little sleepy."

The ride home over the hills and up the country roads was refreshing after the heat and cigarette smoke of the "ballroom." Mrs. Duder made a pot of tea and opened a tin of biscuits while Margaret and I put Edwin to bed. "Too bad Cay wasn't with us tonight. He would have loved it. And the amount of cigarettes he smokes, he would have laughed hearing about the woman who had a five-room bungalow built across the road for her husband to go over there and smoke. She wouldn't let him smoke in the house because the smoke would ruin her lamp shades and drapes. Imagine building another house for your husband to smoke in."

"Tea's served," called Mrs. Duder. We sat and sipped and chatted a little. Margaret said to her mother, "Ed really had a good time tonight."

"Yes," replied Mrs. Duder, "but whatever they put in that punch didn't agree with him."

Margaret went in and turned the light on and removed the bedspread. "Okay, Mom, your bed is all ready."

"Good night, girl," I heard her reply.

Then Margaret said to me, "You know Ed is in love with you, don't you?"

"I know we get along well, because we have the same interests. He writes poetry and I enjoy writing stories and articles. We always have something to talk about. He does not like growing flowers or gardening like Caywood does. I can talk about roses and the outdoors to him. I have often wondered why he never married. He was away from home and on his own for years."

"Jessie and I have often wondered who the little girl in the picture on his desk is, but we never ask questions."

"There must have been a woman in his life, sometime, somewhere. Perhaps that is why he is so quiet. Memories."

24

*W*e were now knee-deep in June. Letters and telephone calls from Edwin were more frequent. He was still talking of sending his mother on a vacation. She wouldn't go the year before. Her excuse was there would be no one to take care of her boys, if she went to visit in Boston. Edwin was loyal to his family but also trying to assert himself, establish a little independence.

Medine and Tony had been in Maine for weeks getting their cottages ready for the summer tourists. They were sorry that they missed the Fireman's Ball. They were not surprised that Margaret had made such a hit with Miles Fletcher. Medine said, "It's too bad she is not interested in him. He would be a good catch. He owns lots of property and has money."

"He's ten years older, and she thinks that is too much of a difference," I replied. Wilmot was ten years older than me. He was a lot more settled in his ways. He didn't believe in wasting time. He always said writing was a waste of time. Every man is different. Wilmot liked raising vegetables and doing things around the house. His only relaxation was smoking his pipe. He always looked so handsome and relaxed when he sat smoking his pipe.

As I was going out to work one morning, the telephone rang. It was Edwin. He said, "I want to have a serious talk with you. We have to be alone. I think you know what I want to say. If I come up on the train next Sunday or Monday, would you pick me up at the station so we could spend the whole day together? I would go back to New York on the eight o'clock train that night. That is, if you wouldn't mind taking me back to Hartford. Just think, we can have a whole day alone."

I drove to work thinking about the telephone conversation. Would I ever remarry? Would I marry and keep on working, or keep on working and not get married again? The joint income of two middle-aged people would undoubtedly result in a higher standard of living. But that in itself should not be a decisive factor in motivating marriage between any age groups. There is something else that is more important: a mutual liking, not necessarily love. Liking a person of the opposite sex is, in some respects, a more durable emotion. I also thought of my work as a librarian. It was pleasant working with friendly people. Books and people complement each other in the most surprising ways. It would be almost axiomatic to say, "Tell me what he reads, and I'll tell you what he is."

The next day there was a letter from Edwin. Again he talked about getting his mother to go to Boston, and about coming up on the train the next week. She wouldn't like that Edwin was going anyplace without her. He said he didn't think it was wise for me to be living alone in such an isolated spot. He thought I needed a man to protect me. He also thought I should get another dog. There were many strangers fishing in the brook, trespassing to be sure, but they were there in the daytime while I was away, and could break in or be in the house when I got home. He did succeed in making me a little apprehensive.

It brought to mind something that had happened a year or so earlier. I had returned home one Monday afternoon after visiting brother Bill and Mary in Medford, Massachusetts, and was surprised to find the remains of food spilled on the dining room table. The cushions on the divan, which were always fluffed up, had the imprint of somebody's head and body. When I went down to the store to get some milk, I mentioned it to Tom Leahy. He wasn't surprised, and said, "That must be the same person who got into Carter's house last week. Nothing was taken. Somebody ate and slept there. Get yourself another dog."

I went home and cleaned up the sticky substance off the table. It looked like gravy or soup. Whoever used the table must have spilled his food and just wiped away the bulk of the spill. I considered myself lucky. What if a gang had gotten in and ruined the divan or the bedspreads or spilled food on the good rugs?

I had walked around outside that night before going to bed. But I was used to walking around outside occasionally, and to having the kitchen door open to get a breath of air when the house was unbearably stuffy. I did not appreciate this new intrusion into my peaceful evenings.

A summer breeze sings sweetly now
Through swaying tree and blossomed bough,
While morning flames in beauty, and,
A curfew tolls in Elfinland.

And I am merry like a child who walks
Where hills are playful, 'cause an echo talks.

Sing on, O breeze, carol a song
Of summer days so warm and long;

Of twilight louvered with the light
Of fireflies on the brink of night.

For I am merry like a child who hears
A bullfrog croaking bedtime prayers.

25

Time has a passion for anonymity, and the years slipped by almost unnoticed. It had been two years since Mac left the house for the last time. Tom and Joan had a baby girl named Linda. They came to visit whenever they could and I went down to Milford, Connecticut, to see them. Friends and relatives made frequent visits and I went to Boston occasionally. Medine and Tony, and Mary and Frank came often, and I had lunch with other friends when they came to Hartford shopping.

Everything followed a peaceful routine. I was becoming an accepted member of our rural community. One day a woman came out from Hartford to visit me. She said her father had become too feeble to carry on as editor of the *Lure of the Litchfield Hills* magazine, and he asked her to talk to me about taking over the editorship and publishing of the magazine. I asked her what the duties would entail.

She said, "Dad thinks you are the one who should take over the magazine because you work with books, and you would have the experience."

"I'm flattered to think your father considers me capable of such an undertaking, but I don't have any magazine experience."

"You would be able to edit and publish it," she insisted, "and the printer will teach you how to do the layout and paste-up. Dad has the mailing list, and the list of stores where the magazine is sold. I would do it myself, but I have kids, I work every day and I have to care for Dad. It isn't too hard. I've helped him with it."

"I work too," I told her.

"You can still keep your job," she said. "Dad has had the magazine for twenty years. He has enjoyed it immensely. I hope you will consider it." And she left for home.

I did do a lot of thinking about it. It was an excellent magazine. Would I be able to do it justice? Would I have the time?

While the idea of becoming an editor and publisher was running around in my head, I received a telephone call from one of the politicians in town offering me the job of registrar of voters. There was no thinking to be done about that job. I declined the offer gracefully by recommending a friend. She was more politically oriented and welcomed the opportunity for close association with the electorate.

On my next day off, I made an appointment with the printer of the magazine, Mr. William Simmers, at the Dowd Printing Company in Winsted. He told me about the work involved, and he said he would be happy to teach me layout and paste-up. The magazine was published four times a year and was nonprofit. The only rewards would be the prestige of heading an historical magazine of such quality, and meeting the people who wrote the articles, plus a working relationship with the distinguished members of the advisory board. The dummy of the magazine had to be at the printers two months before the release date, with the assorted pictures from which cuts had to be made. I thanked him and said I would let him know within a week.

The next time Edwin called, I told him about the magazine

and the visit to the printer. He was delighted and said he would do the proofreading. Then he added, "Wait until you hear the good news I have for you. Mom is going to Cape Cod with the girls. Margaret is coming down this week to get her and, guess what? I'm coming up for a whole day by myself."

"How did you manage that?"

"It wasn't easy. She didn't think we could manage by ourselves. I told her we were big boys now and could surely survive for a week. She gave in reluctantly."

I was at the station waiting for the 10:10 train from New York. Edwin jumped off the steps as happy as a kid who just got out of school for summer vacation. Going down the stairs to the parking lot, he talked nervously.

"Here I am for a whole day. If I had gone home to Long Island to get the car, I wouldn't have made it. Most of the morning would be gone. I hope you don't mind driving me back to the station tonight."

"You must be sleepy," I said.

"Not too bad. I napped on the way up. And will probably do the same going back."

It was a happy, wonderful day. After lunch, we drove up to the Barkhamsted Reservoir and took pictures. Edwin talked mostly about middle-aged people getting married, how much they had to offer each other, the companionship, the experience.

I asked, "How could you get married? You wouldn't leave the family."

"You could sell your property and come live with us."

"Now that is a man talking. You have no idea of how a woman's mind works. There is no kitchen large enough for two women. A woman likes to do things in her own way, and not have another woman standing there watching and offering unsolicited advice. Right or wrong, every woman has her own ideas of keeping house."

He squeezed my hand and said, "I think it deserves a little consideration, don't you?"

On the way back from Barkhamsted, we stopped in at Bud Rainey's farm. I wanted to tell him that I felt badly about the recent loss of his pigs. He was cleaning up the debris. He had to burn the pig pens and everything connected with the pigs.

"What happened?" asked Edwin. "How could hogs get a disease in such a beautiful, clean environment?"

"Damned if I know," replied Bud. "The fellows from the agriculture department came out from Hartford to inspect the farms and they discovered the disease. Over a thousand of them had to be destroyed. It seems a shame. Those little shoats were so damn cute."

"How many animals did you have?" Edwin asked.

"Over a thousand," replied Bud. "It doesn't take long to build up a pig farm. Most of the sows have a litter twice a year, and each litter consists of four to ten piglets, sometimes more. I'd invite you in for tea, only I don't know how to cook anything. The missus is down in Collinsville getting her hair done."

"We have to go home and get supper," I said. "Then I'm taking Edwin back to Hartford to get the train. So long for now."

On the way back to the house, Edwin asked, "How do they do away with over a thousand pigs?"

I explained to him that the men from the agricultural department killed the animals with an injection. Then they had to be buried in a bulldozed pit. And no more hog raising would be allowed on that farm for two years.

"I pity the poor people who have to depend on farming for a living. Fortunately, Bud isn't in that position. What was the disease they had?"

"The deadly swine cholera," I replied.

I drove Edwin back to Hartford after supper. The train left for New York at nine o'clock. He liked working the midnight shift. Caywood didn't go to work until the afternoon, so they could go out in the boat every morning in the summer weather. He gave me a little peck on the cheek and said, "I'll be up again soon."

26

*O*ne night I awoke with the feeling that someone had placed a hand on the edge of the bed. I thought at first it was the new dog, a neglected little waif I had brought home a few days before. The people didn't want her because she was pregnant. They wouldn't let her in the house, and she was half starved, her bones showing through her small frame. I put my hand out to pat her, but she wasn't there. I didn't put the light on. I thought she just moved to another part of the floor near the foot of the bed. She always stayed near me. I figured the poor little thing was uncomfortable and had to move about.

The next thing I knew, I was walking along a street with Wilmot. He would stop in the midst of the crowd, put his arm around me, kiss me, and say how much he missed me. It was an odd gathering; everybody ignored everybody else, and when the cars and trucks came along, nobody moved, the traffic went completely over them, and the people kept right on walking. We walked and talked, and went into an expensive salon where he bought me a blue suit and a white velvet blouse. The salesgirl suggested a lipstick to match the suit, a bluish-pink color. Wilmot watched while I changed into the new clothes and applied the lipstick. Nobody paid the bill; we just strolled out of the store leaving my old things behind. This time there was a familiar face in the crowd. It belonged to Deirdre.

Wilmot remarked, "Deirdre must be here for some television work." We walked to a restaurant with her and ordered something to eat while standing around, for in this place, wherever it was, nobody sat. We ate some kind of strange food and again returned to the crowded street. I asked Wilmot if he was coming home.

"You know I can't do that. You have to come here to me. I'm waiting for you. I'm lonesome for you." Some of the people nearby started looking at their watches. He said, "It is ten minutes to seven, we have to start back. I have to get you home by seven."

At that moment I suddenly awoke and looked at the clock. It was seven on the dot. The glass of water on the night table was almost empty, about half an inch in the bottom.

I couldn't go to work that morning. I called and said I wasn't feeling well. There was no way I could shake off the dream. I walked around outside. I turned on the radio, but I couldn't come back from wherever I was during the night. Do people leave their private, psychic environment for brief intervals, and go wandering out of themselves? Do the dead come back and take you with them on temporary strolls during the night? I was almost persuaded that such was the case.

Medine came up alone that night. Tony was working. We talked about the inexplicable things that happen to people, and were now happening to me. We were both at a loss for a solution to my somewhat ghostly experience.

Again that night I was back in the same city. Everything was the same as the night before—the same people, the same restaurant, the same hurrying home before seven in the morning. There was no more shopping; I was wearing the same new clothes we bought in the other dream. For three nights, the same thing happened with terrifying realism. Once again I talked to Medine about it. She wanted me to come and stay with them for a while. But there was no sense in running away. I had to learn what was the matter with me. I wasn't taking any medication. I wasn't imagining things.

I called and made an appointment to see Mr. Angell, the minister. "Come in and tell me about these dreams. My wife said you called and told her you were terribly upset about dreams you were having."

"I told Margaret I would like to talk to you, if you had the time. For three nights the same thing has happened. And three mornings I wake at exactly the same time. Seven on the dot."

"Sit over here and be comfortable. We will go over everything that has happened." He pulled out a wing chair for me.

He encouraged me to tell him in detail about the dreams, about myself, about my activities, and my work. Then he said, "The only thing the matter with you is you're alone too much. You have never lived in the country before. It is quiet up there. There are no neighbors around."

I reminded him that the Fergusons lived on the next property.

"Well, that's not the same as looking out and seeing lights in another house at night. You are still a young woman. You should get married again. God didn't mean for people to live by themselves. Start thinking about something else. Try to get this out of your mind. By the way, I heard in the store the other day that there is a man from New York coming up to see the widow down by the brook. How about that?"

I told the minister about Edwin, and that he had gotten away by himself this last couple of times on the train. He left New York as soon as he got out of work in the morning, and I picked him up at the station in Hartford.

"How old is he?" asked Mr. Angell.

"Forty-four."

"And he is not married. Has he ever been married?"

"No. He has never had a steady girlfriend. All he did all his life is write poetry. This is the first job he has ever had. He works for Universal Pictures editing film for the movies."

"Is he manly? If he hasn't had girlfriends, how about men friends?"

"He is a shy, gentle person, but there are not many people with as much personality. I don't think he has ever said a mean word or done anything to hurt anybody in his life."

Mr. Angell asked, "Do you suppose he's had some secret love affair? Some woman jilted him? That would make him bitter and shy away from women. I can't understand why such a charming person never married."

"His brother is not married either," I said.

"How about the rest of his family?"

"He has two sisters," I replied, "both married. The older girl married secretly. She told the mother about it when the fellow moved to New Jersey, and she wanted to go to New Jersey to work in a hospital and become a nurse. The mother outfitted her with uniforms and all the necessities and they went to stay at the mother's sister's house in New Jersey. A few days after they arrived, a young man came to the door. He said he came to get his wife. Mrs. Duder said, 'You must be mistaken. You have the wrong house. We don't know your wife.' 'Jessie is my wife.' There was a scene. The mother told Jessie to take her things and 'Get out with the creature, whoever he is.' She never wanted to see her again.

"She didn't speak to Jessie again until Fred, the husband, started running around with other women, and finally left his wife and baby. The mother heard about it from Margaret, Edwin's other sister, and she went to see Jessie and took the child home with her. Then Jessie got a job and a divorce."

"How about the sister Margaret?" asked Mr. Angell.

"She married well. Had a church wedding, six bridesmaids, big reception, and lived in a mansion with a staff. She even hired a maid to take the baby out in the afternoons. But that was short-lived. While she was on vacation one Christmas, she received a telegram from her husband telling her not to come home. He had sold everything, his business, the house, and even the silver they got for wedding presents. She told me, 'He got another woman in trouble. If he didn't get a divorce and marry her, the woman's father was going to sue him. She was a young woman, not yet twenty.' So he skipped town. Another daughter and her baby for a mother to worry about. It sounds like a soap opera."

Mr. Angell said, "You have known the family a long time."

"I went to school with the girls," I replied.

"So, the mother is trying to hold on to Edwin."

"Yes, it's a shame. A person with so much charisma should be out having a good time, enjoying himself, instead of taking his mother shopping, to church, or visiting relatives, or taking the nuns out for an afternoon drive. He has never had a life of his own. I think poetry is his release for emotions, frustrations, disappointments and everything else."

"Will you and he come and see me the next time he comes up from New York?"

"Thank you for seeing me, Mr. Angell. We will come."

I did try to get the dreams out of my mind, but I could not. Each night when I went to bed, I wondered if I was going to die soon and Wilmot was waiting for me. Or if he was trying to tell me something. Did he really take me to that strange place three nights in a row?

I made a whelping box in the coach house for the dog. She would get used to it by the time she had the pups. But I kept her in the house with me at night.

One day I stopped in the Canton Center store on the way home. I overheard a woman saying to Tom Leahy, "I hope they catch him before dark. It would be terrible to have him roaming around in the woods tonight."

"Did you lose your dog?" I asked.

"Oh, no," she replied. "Tom Jones, over across the highway, went out of his mind today and tried to kill his family with a butcher knife. His father is wounded, but not badly. He will recover. But Tom got away from the men who were trying to hold him. He is out there roaming around and he still has the knife with him. The state troopers are looking for him."

I hurried home. It was getting dark. I couldn't decide if it was better to leave all the lights on outside for protection, or if having the lights on would attract him to the door. I decided to keep the dog in and the lights out.

27

*A*nother eventful year slipped by. More exciting things were happening every day, and perhaps the most exciting of all was the arrival in town of Bob Andrews and his wife, Margaret. They were truly a dynamic pair, and shared an abiding interest in the theater which was soon given tangible form when they rented the Canton Show Shop that had been closed for years. It had originally been the coach house for a large estate. Now, with its well-lighted proscenium stage, conspicuous under the open-beamed ceiling, it was once again ready to present its weekly programs. This time, the actors and actresses would be professionals from Broadway and Hollywood.

The fringe benefits of my new status as editor and publisher were gradually extended to me. I was among the first to be invited to a cocktail party launching the opening. I accepted with pleasure. Once again I wore the blue dress and accessories. It was a beautiful Sunday afternoon. Prominent members of suburban society were well represented, the men in formal wear and the women in beautiful gowns. I arrived unaccompanied. I stood in the front lobby holding a glass of ginger ale, which looked exactly like the cocktail it was presumed to be. Couples were standing around in groups boisterous with chatter and merriment. It was then that the first surprise in my new career occurred. Everett Horton, or Edward Everett Horton, as he was billed in the program, strolled in unannounced. For some unknown reason, the movie star came right toward me, grasped my hand and kissed me heartily on the cheek. I was flabbergasted, but managed to whisper, "You must have mistaken me for someone else." His only response was to take me by the arm and start walking across the lobby to a sofa.

When we were seated, he said, "I'm alone, will you stay with me? That is, if you are here alone."

Bob Andrews looked a little puzzled as he commented, "I was about to introduce you two."

"As you see, there's no need to," said Mr. Horton, with that impish grin which so long endeared him to numerous fans. "We have already met."

Altogether, it proved to be an exciting party. Mr. Horton had come from California to star in the opening presentation, *A White Sheep in the Family*. He remained all summer, and was in several plays. We spent many hours together. Other stars followed, many of them household names, and were soon added to my growing roster of new friends. Two of the most memorable were, and are, Richard and Beryl Durham. Beryl came to the United States from Wales. She had the most beautiful speaking voice a person could possess. Richard is an American, from the Midwest. He had contracted to play in the *Happiest Millionaire, Diabolique* and *Bus Stop*. Beryl appeared in Dylan Thomas's *Under Milkwood*. Their performances were superb. Richard's histrionic talent owed much to his magnificent, rich-textured, resonant voice. He used it as one would use a violin and was able to project nuances of sound and meaning that never failed to enthrall audiences.

As my friendship with the Durhams ripened, I sought in

various ways to make their stay in Canton as pleasant as possible. I suggested that they spend their available free time at my place, where the children could frolic in the brook while we adults enjoyed the privacy and coolness of a place in the country. It made me happy to see them happy. I shall always be grateful for having such wonderful friends.

The end of the theatrical season was almost traumatic. I had become so involved in writing reviews of the plays, that it had become difficult for me to maintain an objective approach. I liked most of the plays. However, my melancholy was short-lived. I consoled myself with the thought that the Show Stop would be presenting plays again next summer.

Autumn slipped quietly by. Nothing much happened. A friend whom I hadn't seen in months came in the library one day. She told me her husband had turned over a new leaf. He gave up drinking and woman chasing, and had even started going to church Sundays—then he dropped dead. It was one of those sad and funny things, almost like the jokes we hear on the television or radio.

The week before Christmas, Edwin called to tell me his mother would like me to spend the Christmas holiday weekend with them. I had spent Thanksgiving with Tom and Joan, and was able to accept the invitation without feeling guilty about not being with the children for Christmas. There were no storms predicted, so I drove down to Long Island. Before setting out for the weekend, I went over to Fyler's Christmas tree farm in Simsbury and cut a beautiful little blue spruce to take to Mrs. Duder. I knew she would have room for a table tree. We had a delightful evening decorating the tree and wrapping gifts. Jessie, her new husband, Frank, and Margaret came from Boston on the train. It was a happy yuletide reunion.

Before I left for home, the day after Christmas, Mrs. Duder said, "Mary, girl, I would like to have a little chat with you while the boys are gone to the store."

"Great," I replied.

She continued, "I know Edwin is fond of you. I know he goes up to Hartford on the train. I wouldn't mind him marrying a single woman. I mean, a woman who doesn't have a family."

"I am a single woman. A widow is a single woman."

"But, what I mean is, girl, you have children and grandchildren. And Edwin has never had any responsibility. He has never had to worry about money or anything. He always has been with me."

"I'm not anxious to marry anyone," I replied. "I'm getting along fine. I have a nice job, and I do some things for the newspapers. I enjoy writing."

"I got nothing against you, girl, it's just that Edwin should not get married. He's over forty years old and settled in his ways. He's better off the way he is. He has me to take care of him. Don't get me wrong, girl. Come down and visit when you can. We enjoy having you. And we will go up to the country. It's like another world up there. I've often wondered how you could stand the loneliness. The place is so isolated, with no neighbors to drop in."

"I don't have time to be lonely," I replied.

Driving home, I couldn't help thinking about what she said: 'not a neighbor to drop in.' There weren't any friends or neighbors dropping in, and that was a neighborhood of houses on fifty-foot lots. You could see the woman in the next house standing at the sink. And why didn't the men ever bring a friend home? Two handsome men who just went out to work, and came home from work or to their boat. It was difficult for me to understand a mother keeping her sons under her domination. They really had dull lives. At that point I stopped speculating. Besides, it was none of my business.

Safe back at home, I had just poured my second cup of tea when the telephone rang. Tom and Joan were checking up to see if I had gotten home safely, and if I had enjoyed my visit to New York. Then Bill and Billie called from San Diego to wish me a Happy Christmas. They said they had telephoned the night before to no avail, and wanted to know where I had been. I said I would tell them about it later in a letter.

The next morning I went to the kennel in North Canton to pick up my new little dog, Buster. He was one of the litter the poor mother dog had. She died, and I gave the puppies away, all except Buster. A woman who worked there said, "We had some excitement in town while you were away."

"What kind of excitement?" I asked.

"There is a man dressed in women's clothes driving around at night. He flashes his lights to signal women drivers to pull over. When they stop their cars, he attacks and rapes them. His first victim was found unconscious on West Mountain Road. Good thing someone came along and found her. Otherwise, she might have frozen to death, being half naked as she was."

I assured the woman that I would not be out at night, except on Thursdays when the library was open until nine. On those nights I didn't get home until ten. There would always be the uneasy feeling that he might be hiding in the woods.

The rapist had not been apprehended and the state troopers were baffled. Then another series of rapes occurred in Simsbury. The assailant used different tactics this time. He dressed as a woman, but no longer stopped cars at night. His rapes were committed in the homes of his victims while their husbands were at work. Efforts to identify him continued around the clock. Local people helped as much as they could. Strangers in town were observed closely, and any unusual or suspicious incident was reported immediately. There was even talk that Canton should have a police officer of its own. The state trooper was overburdened by too much responsibility.

In the latter part of January, Edwin called and said he would like to come up for a day. I told him I was nervous now about being out alone at night. It would be better if he waited until the evenings were light. He said, "You won't be alone. I'll be with you."

"You will be with me going into Hartford, but I will have

to drive back home alone." When I told Medine and Tony that Edwin wanted to come up for a day and I discouraged him, Tony said, "What did you do that for? We will take him back to the station any night." Edwin was delighted to hear of Tony's offer and said he would be up on his next day off.

When he did arrive, his first greeting was "I've been thinking you should sell your property and move to Hartford or, better still, come to New York."

"I could never leave my place. That house is like a legacy. It is a house that was built to be my home—a place to live independently of children and relatives."

"You need someone to look after you," said Edwin. "You shouldn't be up here in the woods alone. It is not like it was a few years ago."

"I've learned to take care of myself," I replied. "But I am thinking about another job, perhaps just working freelance for the newspapers. Years ago I was never nervous. I often walked down to the brook in the moonlight."

Edwin's only contribution to this dialogue was "I don't think I've ever gone home to an empty house."

We didn't stop at the Canton Center store, we went straight home from the station. Edwin's next remark proved that he had been reviewing my situation. "You won't have to look for another job."

"Why not?"

"Because we could get married, and then you could rent the property, if you don't wish to sell it, and come to live with us."

"That's something that would require serious thinking."

"You will probably stop thinking and start doing one of these days," he replied, somewhat curtly, I thought.

Shortly after this latest date with Edwin, I had a rather unnerving experience. Early one Monday afternoon, there was a knock on the front door. Whoever it was didn't ring the bell. That in itself made me suspicious. The knocking continued but I decided not to respond. Instead I went into the front bedroom and peeped out through the side of the drapes. I was in time to see a tall, muscular-looking 'woman' walking by the window. She, or he, then got into a black VW that was parked a few feet up from the driveway, and drove up the road. I was unable to see the license number. However, my identification of the car, color and make helped the state troopers put an end to the crimes. A few weeks later, the rapist was trapped while parked near the home of another potential victim.

Another welcome spring arrived followed by a hot, humid summer. I received an invitation to attend the writer-reader conference which was held the last week of June every year at the Suffield Academy in Suffield, Connecticut. I called Mrs. Frances Edwards to thank her for the invitation. She said, "Be sure to come for the opening party Sunday afternoon and bring a friend."

Edwin was delighted when I called and told him about the conference. He said, "I'll drive up early Sunday and take the family with me. They can amuse themselves while you and I go to Suffield."

We had a delightful time that Sunday. The rest of the week I went over alone, but Edwin came back for the closing party the following Sunday. We met Padraic Colum, the famous Irish poet and folklorist; Stephen Spender, English poet at the Library of Congress; Louis Untermeyer, lecturer; Jacques Cartier, founder and director of the Hartford Stage Company; William J. Smith, poet and playwright; and Roger Eddy, American novelist. Edwin and Padraic Colum were attracted to each other immediately. The closing Sunday, as we were walking up the steps to the academy, Padraic was coming down. As we shook hands, he quoted two lines from one of Edwin's poems. That was the biggest thrill in Edwin's life, and he admitted it. "When I write some of my friends and tell them I met, and talked to, Padraic Colum, they won't believe it."

Not long after that memorable week I received a letter from New York, but this one was not from Edwin, it was from Caywood. It read:

Dear Mary,

Just thought I would drop you a few lines during an idle moment to tell you how much I enjoy going up to see you and walking in the woods by the brook and even catching a trout or two. Ed is not home yet. It is nine a.m. Mom is busy doing this and that, here and there. The cat is out in the yard. Mom won't let him in the house. The flowers are lovely, the weather is beautiful, and you are lovely too. So, all's right in the world. Yesterday was warm. Ed and I sat in the boat, tied up at the dock, and soaked our feet, and let the sun tan our hides. Needless to say, our thoughts were of you. Always I think of you, when I go near the sea, and watch the cabin cruisers go by, and picture you there sailing down Sunshine Bay. I can see you now, with a gold braided cap, white shoes, white pants, and gold buttons on your jacket, standing there at the wheel, tall and straight, keeping a weather eye to the leeward. The gentle summer breeze playing with a wisp of hair floating free, and dancing in the sun, and your heart in tune with the song of the gulls, wild and free. The glint of silver on the rippling waves, and the carefree laughter of one at peace with the world. When the mind wanders, what lovely pictures we paint. Like a glimpse into paradise and so now I come back to our everyday world, and say Ed is looking for a letter from you everyday. I know you are busy, and on the go. If you ever get a breathing spell, drop us a word or two, just so we will know you are still there, and give an account of yourself. Sometime in October we will all be up to see you, and now, shipmate, anchors away and adieu,

As ever, Cay

What a beautiful letter. It brought a lump to my throat. It seemed Caywood was doing some thinking for himself too. Perhaps, someday, he will be driving off for a day with a friend. She will be a lucky woman.

There was another letter in the mail that day. It was from

the American Cancer Society requesting that I volunteer my services as a public relations person conducting the publicity for the cancer drives. I called the chairman and promised to do what I could to help promote the campaign. I worked with Mrs. Lodge, the governor's wife, doing the paperwork.

During the month of October the weather was crisp with the leaves changing color. The woods were carpeted with red, orange, brown and the dark yellow of the sugar maples. The Sunday that my friends came from both Long Island and Boston, another farm incident happened. We were having our lunch when a neighbor over on Highway 179 called to give me a news tip. One of Carl Dewey's cows had caught her head between the strands of barbed-wire fencing while munching the greener grass on the outside. In her struggle to free herself, the wire cut deeply into her throat. When the veterinarian arrived, she was dead. He performed a cesarean on the spot and saved the calf. When I told Carl I was sorry that he had lost such a valuable Jersey, his reaction was philosophical. "It's all in a day's work," he replied.

"How will they feed a motherless calf?" asked Mrs. Duder.

"I didn't ask Carl but I imagine they will feed it on a bottle, like they do with sheep," I said.

Jessie asked, "With all the pasture they have, why do cows stick their heads out through a fence to eat the grass outside it, especially a pregnant cow? She should be lying down in a nice, cool field."

Edwin laughed. "There's no accounting for what females do."

Jessie ignored the comment. "Where are we going from here?" she continued.

"Let's be a little more cheerful," said Edwin. "Talking about one farmer losing his barn, all the hay stored in the silo, as well as his farm machinery, and now this young man losing his valuable cow, talking about cows and milk, is there any-place where we could get a nice ice cream soda?"

Margaret said, "Eddie, all you think about is your gut. Forget the ice cream and let's go look at some old, historic houses."

We drove down Route 44 and stopped in front of the Phoebe Humphrey house, a saltbox colonial built in 1759. It had over twelve windows and a huge stone chimney. In recent years the owners had rented rooms to tourists. Some of the Show Shop people stayed there. An old tree, called the Revolutionary tree, shaded the terraced garden, which seemed to be growing out of the side of the mountain. Mr. Bristol, who was working at the side of the house, noticed us and came to the car.

"Hello, Mrs. MacNeill. I see you got company from the city." I introduced him to everybody. "Would you like to take a look around the house? It is quiet today, nobody home."

We followed him in the front door. He told the story about the house a little differently than the way I had already heard it, but coming from him it was like a trip into the historic past.

He said, "Phoebe Humphrey was born in this house in 1763. The year Phoebe was born, the country was in rebellion against the British. Her father, Master Sam, was lame and unfit for military service. He taught school and instilled in the minds of his children the principles that underlie republican government. She was thirteen years old when the Declaration of Independence was signed. And one day when Phoebe was sixteen years old, her father was away teaching and her mother and the rest of the children were up the hill in the berry field. Phoebe was left alone to bake bread, and her mother warned her to 'look out for the bread and herself.' It had been reported that British soldiers had been seen in another part of town the night before. Phoebe was watching the bread when she was surprised by soldiers. One of them demanded some bread while a tall, handsome one ransacked the pantry. She refused to give them anything. As she parleyed with the soldiers, she noticed the heavy iron poker in the fireplace. She snatched the red-hot poker from the fire, swung it over her head like a saber and bade them 'be gone.' The soldiers did not stop to pick up the bread or anything else. They ran out of the house, up the highway, and into the woods. Phoebe had not only saved her bread, but won herself and family honors."

"What an exciting story," said Margaret.

As we toured the house, Mrs. Duder remarked, "What beautiful floors and woodwork."

"Most of the building material was cut from trees on the property, and the rest of it was brought down the mountain at the back of the house. Other lumber was cut and sawed for sheathing, floorboards, and so on," said Mr. Bristol.

"How did they get the water in the house years ago?" asked Caywood.

"The water came from the same spring up the mountain, but it now has modern pipes instead of the old wooden logs with holes drilled or burned through them."

"Where is the well?" asked Edwin. Mr. Bristol escorted the men around to the back of the house to the well house and showed them the enormous flagstones used in the walk to the kitchen door. He told them about the old English bricks worked into the fireplace, and the original Phoebe Humphrey kettle and crane in the Dutch oven.

Jessie and her husband were amazed that a house could be so well preserved after all those years. "Just think, Frank, this house is over two hundred years old, and it looks nicer than the new houses."

"I can hear the birds outside the kitchen window calling 'Phoebe, Phoebe, Phoebe,'" said Mrs. Duder.

The granite boulder on Phoebe's grave was carried down from her mountain, and the inscription on it reads, "My strength and my flesh faileth, but God is the strength of my heart and my portion forever."

We thanked Mr. Bristol and went back home to get supper, but the excitement of the old house seemed to fill us with emotion. Even Edwin had lost his appetite.

"There is so much history to be learned," said Caywood. "Every time we come to Canton Center, we learn something. We must come back soon, before winter sets in."

"I'm glad I didn't have to keep house in those days," said Margaret.

"Me too," smiled Jessie. "Imagine baking and cooking in a Dutch oven. Frank wouldn't have to worry about dieting. We would starve to death."

When the good-byes were said, Edwin kissed me on the cheek, a more lingering kiss than usual. "I'll be back soon and alone. I want to have a serious talk with you."

28

I did a lot of thinking, and also a lot of listening. What I thought and what I heard were frequently in conflict. That is usually the way when one is trying to arrive at a momentous decision. One tries to be logical about things, to keep the emotional side of one's nature from interfering with the making of an objective analysis of relevant data.

When I talked to friends and relatives in Massachusetts about remarrying, they were full of advice, well meaning, to be sure. "You ought to start living for yourself now. For years you have been wife, nurse and wage-earner. Those were hard, difficult, heartbreaking years. We often wondered how you managed to escape a breakdown. Buy yourself a new wardrobe. Travel." How easy it all sounded, but living only for oneself is actually not living at all.

When I told Medine about the well-meaning counsel I had received from friends, she said, "They were concerned, and worried lest you make a mistake."

I agreed that such a possibility existed, but said that I was optimistic. "Why shouldn't I be? Edwin is such a wonderful person, so much charisma, and he is kind, considerate and sober. He only takes a few drinks at a party. He is not too ambitious in regard to making, or saving, money, I will admit. He says money is something to be used to buy what you want." But my biggest concern was, how would he make the break? How would his mother take it? I was not worried about him getting work in Hartford. He had already proposed, and was expecting an answer the next time he came up.

Medine smiled as she listened. "You don't have to convince me. I'm prejudiced. I like Edwin myself."

"There are other considerations," I said. "When a man has been a bachelor, and never away from home, or mother, how does he adjust to responsibility? His mother said he was too set in his ways to get married."

Few marriages, I'm sure, were ever approached with more circumspection, or with a more conscientious deploying of pros and cons. While all this inner turmoil was turmoiling, I received encouragement from the children. They thought it would be the wisest, happiest choice I could make. They loved Edwin. They said it would make them happy for me to have someone to love and care for me, someone for companionship.

The next time Edwin came up, I showed him the letters. He grinned. "I'm not here to read letters, nor palms, nor tea leaves, nor cards. I'm here on this special occasion for one particular purpose. I want an answer to the most courageous question I ever asked."

When he finally settled down to reading the letters, his comments were as visible as some of the letters' contents. He said, "The trouble with advice, solicited or unsolicited, is that those who give it so abundantly are rarely as sagacious as they think they are. Those who advise us to marry, and those who advise us not to marry, can be equally sincere, and equally wrong. Socrates was much less equivocal when he said, 'Whether you marry, or do not marry, you'll regret it.' Therefore, the time has come for you and I to make our own decision."

He took my face in his hands and asked, "Have you decided on a date?"

"How about May fourteenth," I replied.

Only an artist of superb skill could have captured the expression of surprise on Edwin's face. He put his arm around me and said, "Why, dear, did it take you so long to decide?"

A middle-aged romance that is about to be made permanent through marriage is often beset by obstacles, and ours was no exception. We were both bothered by his mother's continued reluctance to grant her blessing. No doubt, her opposition was not without justification. Her bachelor son, who had never been away from home overnight, was now proposing marriage to a widow and grandmother. Perhaps, if I had been a spinster, she would have been less combative.

We talked to Mr. Angell, and he was delighted. He and Edwin had become friends, and he came up to the house when he knew Edwin was in town. The date of May 14 was reserved for us at seven o'clock in the evening. We then proceeded with the arrangements. It would, we agreed, be a simple affair attended only by relatives and a few friends. Medine and Tony would be the best man and matron of honor.

When we returned to the house from the church, with our small party in tow, we were surprised to find the whole place brilliantly lighted and every room decorated with freshly cut spring flowers. It was a heart-warming, unforgettable sight, a finale that had been carefully planned by Natalie and Bob who were waiting to greet us as we entered. The place was literally bulging with people, friends as well as friends of friends.

Edwin was astounded. "It looks," he said, "more like a fete than a reception." Margaret and Jessie served the wine with portions of the beautifully decorated cake, made by Medine and her sister Bessie. Mrs. Duder sat quietly on the divan.

I went over, took her hand and said, "Don't worry about Edwin. I'm sure he will be happy."

"I'm losing a son," she replied.

Edwin heard this remark and said, "Cheer up, Mom. You're coming on our honeymoon with us."

Margaret, who was just about to offer her mother another glass of wine, took Edwin by the arm. "Mom is coming to Boston with us. I'll see to that. Whoever heard of a mother going along on a honeymoon?"

What a beautiful honeymoon it was: A trip across country, six weeks of sightseeing across the southern route to Texas and San Diego, then to San Francisco, and then the northern route back to Canton Center.

And now, as I put aside this journal-companion, I have no desire to make prognostications about the future. My mood is definitely more philosophic than prophetic. In my own, personal way, I have taken care of the past, and feel that it is not too arrogant to say, "Let the future take care of itself."

A Place in the Country

Down! Down! The sun slopes down
The hills that hedge this little town,
And up those hills, so high and steep,
We watch and hear the shadows creep.
Up! Up! The shadows go,
Leaving darkness far below,
For night has come, and leaves no trace
Of day about this country-place.

Old Farmer Brown has broiled his toes;
Sipped his sugared rum, and goes
Creaking up the muffled stairs
To lose in sleep his dwindling cares.
A wise man he; and will not borrow
Fresh trouble from some dim tomorrow.

Up! Up! Here comes the sun,
As the shadows break and run,
And barking dogs are all about
As roosters crow a clarion shout.
Down! Down! The shadows race
The hills that hide this country-place,
For day has come, and leaves no stain
Of darkness on the window-pane.

Old Farmer Brown is wide awake;
Ready to eat, and eager to rake
The tousled leaves in tidy heaps,
For he is a man who always keeps
Prolific earth in prime condition,
Achieving thus his life's sole mission.

Epilogue

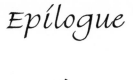

At times, ill health dictates an early retirement. The severe winters and upkeep of a large house and property presents too arduous a task. After twenty-four years, I had to make the decision. Ed was now sick, and I kept telling myself I could no longer take care of the place. It was no longer a question of to move, or not to move; it was definitely to move.

The first step was to sell the house and land. The next, and just as emotional a task, was to find good homes for the pets who had been a part of the family for years.

At the law office for the closing, I felt sad and lonely. It seemed I was leaving Mac behind. The buyer, a doctor, and his wife, a nurse, were talking about their plans for the property. He was going to use the pond for breeding trout. She was talking about the flowers she was going to grow.

I kept thinking about the kind, lovely, caring people in the little town. I would miss them. They were always there when I needed help, always taking care of the place when I went away, or, if something wasn't working, someone would try to fix it.

Would there be another place like this?

The adjustment to life in San Diego was greater than anticipated. Our small house caused endless frustration, and there was no land, just a small lot. We were, however, able to begin our new life in the beautiful, sunny climate. But that new life was not enjoyable for long.

Again, in a couple, one person dies first—usually the husband. Being alone is not living. It is only existing. Every person, animal or thing needs somebody, or some thing.

I bought a lovely holly tree from Florida one year. It was covered with red berries, and healthy-looking. In a short time, it was dead. I asked the local florist about it. He said it was a female tree, and with no other holly tree around, it died. So it seems every person, animal and thing alive needs someone.

There are times, when I'm in the hospital or feeling slight despair, when I feel Mac is still with me. And maybe he knows that at ninety-three years old, I'm still living in my own house, and I have learned to take care of myself.

MARY MACNEILL was born in St. John's, Newfoundland, in 1905. She received her education at the Presentation Convent and St. Clare's Private School for Young Ladies.

Mary was editor and publisher of Connecticut's award-winning magazine *The Lure of the Litchfield Hills,* wrote feature articles and book reviews for the *Hartford Courant,* worked as a librarian in Hartford, Connecticut, self-published five books and taught creative writing.

Mary is a member of the National League of American Pen Women, San Diego Writers and Editors Guild and Connecticut League of Historical Societies. She now lives in San Diego.